WHY BAD GRADES HAPPEN TO GOOD KIDS

WHAT PARENTS NEED TO KNOW — WHAT PARENTS NEED TO DO

Linda Bress Silbert, Ph.D.
Alvin J. Silbert, Ed.D.

BEAUFORT
BOOKS
New York

Why bad grades happen to good kids
by Linda Bress Silbert and Alvin J. Silbert

Published by Beaufort Books, New York
27 West 20th Street
New York, NY 10011

ISBN-13: 978-0-8253-0577-1

Library of Congress Control Number: 2007931244

Illustrations by Bob Berry

10 9 8 7 6 5 4 3 2 1

*To our parents
for pointing us in the right direction;
to our children and grandchildren
for continuing to blaze new trails in that direction.*

Also by the same authors

Strong Learning® Products
Study Skills Workbooks (5 Titles - Grades 6-12)
Creative Thinking Workbooks (7 Titles - Grades K-6)
Beginning Reading Storybooks (8 Titles - Grades 1-4)
Make My Own Book Kits (7 Titles - Grades PreK-1)
Life Skills Program (6 Titles - Grades K-5)
Phonics Card Games (20 Titles - Grades K-6)

For more information, please visit:
www.stronglearning.com
1-888-3-STRONG
1-888-378-7664

Contents

Foreword

by Al Roker

I'm glad you picked up this book. Why? Because it means you care about education and the educational welfare of your own kids. Not everyone does. They may feel it's the job of teachers, principals and the school board.

It's *your* job. You are the parent. Like it or not, the time and effort you put into your child's education impacts considerably what your child will get out of it.

I am addicted to these kinds of books. Guides, quiz books, and curriculum information books have become a huge part of my personal library. The problem with most of these books, however, is that they are based on thinking that goes back to Abe Lincoln writing his homework on the back of a shovel! (How the heck he got the shovel into the printer, I'll never know.)

Why Bad Grades Happen to Good Kids by Drs. Linda and Al Silbert looks at how to help educate your child in a whole new way. I first became familiar with their work when a friend recommended them to me years ago. Their user-friendly approach to helping children was so good, I found that I could actually help my kids. My biggest fear was that as my children were getting older, I would have to go back to school in order to be able to help them with their homework.

If you're my age you probably remember the "new math." It gave my parents fits. They would help me with my homework and it would take hours, because I was using the "new math" while they were using the "old math." I'd end up being more confused than ever. The only thing my folks and I could agree on was that 2+2=4. Anything more than that was up for grabs.

This book gives you an advantage my parents never had. I know at least a dozen parents whose kids were helped by going to the Strong Learning Centers run by Linda and Al. In fact, Linda and Al helped *them* as much as they helped their kids. What's great about their philosophy is that it not only strengthens whatever academic weakness your child has, be it English, science or math, but it takes his or her learning and organizational skills to a new level.

It's interesting that no matter how much we progress, we still remain the same. As a student, I always made the same vow at the beginning of the school year: *I am going to be different this year.* I would get my homework done on time, as soon as I got home. Projects would not be put off till the last minute, and studying for exams would not consist of cramming on the school bus ride the morning of the tests.

The first couple of weeks were always ideal. I turned in assignments on time; I had my loose-leaf binder with dividers for every subject and lots of clean paper with reinforcement rings on the holes. I was an educational ball of fire.

But as the work started piling on and getting harder, those vows would fall by the wayside, one by one, until around Christmas, when I started to look at *next* year as the year that would be the real turning point.

Why Bad Grades Happen to Good Kids will help your child avoid having the same frustrating experience I had. If you are still reading this while you're in the bookstore, close the book, walk to the cash register and buy it. Unlike that computer you purchased to assist your kids with their homework, *this* will actually help. And, as a bonus, they can't use *Why Bad Grades Happen to Good Kids* to play video games or chat with their friends online.

Acknowledgments

We would like to thank David Hicks, Ph.D., Wendy DeGigglio, and Gaye Delcampo for their critical review of the manuscript and helpful comments that helped turn a rough draft into a book. In addition, we would like to thank Cheryl Schnitzer, Ph.D., Patricia DeVine, M.D., and Frank Bariff for reading the first draft and for their valuable suggestions. We would also like to thank the people at Beaufort Books for their assistance, and Vally Sharpe for working so closely with us in the final editing stages. Thanks too to our thousands of clients over the years who have put their trust in us, and, in the process, taught us so much.

Finally, we would like to thank our wonderful children and parents for their support.

Please Note: This book is a guide for parents and other caregivers of children. It is not intended to be the basis of solving serious individual or family problems. As noted throughout this book, in dealing with any crisis or serious situation, we urge you to consult a professional—family physician, psychologist, psychiatrist, family counselor, school counselor, or other professional—as appropriate.

Also note that throughout the text, numerous case studies have been included for illustrative purposes. Student identities have been fictionalized or disguised, and names or other identifying characteristics have been changed.

Introduction

Why Do Bad Grades Happen To Good Kids?

Wouldn't it be nice if this were a multiple choice question? If that were the case, the solution would be easy. Choose an answer, follow the instructions, and voilá, the problem is resolved.

For the sake of family harmony, we wish it were this simple, but of course, it isn't. The reasons for sub-par academic performance are numerous and often intertwined, which means they are often not obvious and, consequently, elusive for the most well-intentioned parent.

Within the pages of this short, easy-to-read book, we've taken a look at virtually all of the possible reasons. Since there is usually more than one reason at play, we've presented them in the form of case studies, so that you can more easily recognize the situations and symptoms and determine if they apply to you and your family.

Each chapter examines academic difficulty in terms of *cause* and *effect*. The reasons are the *causes*, and the bad grades (and the resulting family disharmony) are the *effects*.

Through this book, we offer our extended hand — the benefit of years of experience in helping families understand and solve this very common conundrum. Take it, read it and then read it again, and begin to explore why bad grades may be happening to your good kid. Or, if your child is not yet of school-age, learn what you can do to reduce the chances that the challenge of bad grades will cross your door.... It's our hope that, in a short time, you'll come to know what you need to *know,* and what you need to *do.*

Linda & Al Silbert

Chapter 1

Developing S+T+R+O+N+G Kids

All her mom wanted was for Jessica to be happy.
Jessica — Age 12

The Wilsons had brought Jessica in for an educational evaluation. During our initial consultation, I found myself looking at three unhappy people. All Mom talked about were the piles of incomplete homework and projects, telephone calls, e-mails and notes from teachers, and the yelling and slamming of Jessica's bedroom door. Dad jumped in to describe the fighting between Jessica and her mom. When it was her turn, Jessica revealed that what she hated most was the screaming, the long lectures about school, and the grounding when she did poorly on tests.

The barrage of questions from the Wilsons gave me some insight into the situation. "She used to do so well. What's wrong with her? Does she have ADHD? Are there learning problems we've missed? Is she just lazy? Should we get the computer out of the house so she stops meeting her friends on-line?"

They both remarked that they didn't remember school being like this when they were young. "When I was in seventh grade I came home and played after school. But Jessica has to do homework for hours," Mom said. "I don't remember anything that comes close to the scene in our home every night."

Nightly dramas like Jessica's play out everywhere there are schools and children. Install a video camera into a neighbor's home and there's a good chance you'll see a different scene, but the same play.

Why? The answer is simple. Children need to be prepared to compete in an information-driven global economy, so we've raised the academic bar again and again and again.

In addition, not only do we expect our children to be good students–even *great* students–we also expect them to participate in after-school activities, do community service, babysit their younger siblings, be responsible for various household chores and then deal with piles of homework. The list goes on and on. And the number of hours in a day is still twenty-four. It's enough to stress out any kid. And stressed-out kids sometimes get bad grades.

How to Educate Your Children Without Harming Them or the Well-being of Your Family

All parents dream of giving their children the best education possible so they can live successful and happy lives. But somewhere in the midst of all this schooling this goal is lost, as families become overloaded and anxious about school. It has been our life's work to help such families.

Often, school success — not play, happiness, or family harmony — becomes the exclusive focus of childhood and teen years. This is not entirely bad. After all, our children need to be prepared to enter the workforce with enough skills to land them a good job. What is bad is if their childhood, their teen years, and their futures as young adults — in addition to the well-being of their families — are harmed in the process.

Yet all too often, this is exactly what is happening. As if you didn't have enough to worry about, as a parent you have to now be on your guard to protect your child from the academic frenzy that often results from the well-intentioned but sometimes misguided implementation of new educational standards. So, at this time, we are officially deputizing you. It's now up to you to be vigilant to prevent the new, increased demands of education from driving an ever-widening wedge between you and your child.

As you probably know all too well, this is a difficult task. Parents often become consumed by the day-to-day dynamics of their children's schoolwork and are unable to stand back far enough to retain their objectivity. Moreover, because school problems develop gradually, over a span of many years, and the intensity of the daily schooling experience tends to overshadow everything else, it is easy to lose sight of the big picture. Thus, our advice to all parents who find themselves in this scenario is, for starters, to keep schooling in perspective.

> **Keep schooling in perspective.**

It's your job to help your child get through school, or in some cases just to survive it. But, even more importantly, it's to help your child become an emotionally, socially, and intellectually strong adult who is successful and independent—a good person, one who has a loving, caring relationship with you, with her family, and with her associates. A lofty goal, isn't it? But isn't that what parenting is all about?

You're probably thinking, "Don't we want to also stretch our children's developing minds?" The answer is a resounding "YES!" Of course we do.

We are all laying the bricks for the new age. But in some cases we have forgotten what we are building — not robots, but children. And the sudden shift in curriculum and expanding volume of work for some children becomes overwhelming for them and their families. The piles of papers alone would make the average adult break out in hives! At school, many children feel frustrated, embarrassed, and insecure — and they are terrified of failing. After school, many are transported to day care or to a babysitter, or stay after school for extra help while others run off to some activity such as a Scouts meeting, twirling, soccer or hockey practice, music or karate lessons, religious instruction, therapy, or band rehearsal. Then they rush home to wolf down their dinner and, before the last morsel has been swallowed, they are ordered to tackle their homework. Kids simply cannot handle this kind of a schedule for any length of time without some sort of meltdown. For their own emotional, social, and developmental well being, they need free time to unwind, think, and relax.

Walter — Age 17

Walter squeaked in for an 8:30 p.m. appointment. He couldn't concentrate at all. He asked me if I had anything that could take away his headache. After a brief conversation, it was easy to see why he had a throbbing headache. He awoke at 5:00 A.M. to finish the homework from the day before. After school he had football practice. Then at 5:30 P.M. he rushed to work at the deli where he usually worked until about 9:00. When he got home he started his homework, but usually fell asleep before completing it.

After hearing his schedule, I had a headache! Upon completing the fourth or fifth day of a week's schedule grid, the

"Yikes! I'm all booked up...no time left for school!"

cause of Walter's school problems started to come into focus, even to him. With Walter's full participation, this was
an easy issue to resolve.

Our lifestyles today are very different from that of our
parents. In many cases, Mom and Dad live at the same
hectic pace as their children do. They don't give themselves
much time for their own nurturing activities and relaxation,
so they certainly don't encourage their children to do so.

What to do? While you might not be in a position to
totally revamp your lifestyle, you need to be aware of these
pressures, and institute some small changes so that your
child has time to breathe.

Children—and teens—still need to play. Although
children may be playing computer games now instead of
hopscotch, and teens may be online instead of meeting at
the corner soda shop, in reality, kids are basically the same
today as they ever were. We all need to take an objective
and general approach to our children's development and

keep schooling in perspective. Their schooling is important, even critical, but we need to be careful not to let it destroy their precious years of growth.

Why Children Struggle in School

Children struggle in school for many reasons, but parents, teachers, and other adults tend to focus not on the causes, but on the effects. The result? The struggling student frequently comes across as being lazy, uncaring, and/or having an attitude problem. But when we focus on these issues, we are taking the easy way out, and not dealing with the actual causes.

Usually it takes some investigating to get to the real cause of school problems. But the effort is well worth it.

What are those causes? Invariably, they involve issues in one or more of the following general areas:

Physical issues: hearing loss or poor vision; health issues such as obesity, poor nutrition and sleep deprivation; learning issues associated with brain function such as dyslexia, dysgraphia, language processing, or Attention-Deficit/Hyperactivity Disorder (ADHD or the older term, ADD).

Social issues: peer pressure, poverty, divorce, family problems, school bullies, parental disinterest in education.

Educational issues: difficulty in particular subjects—especially reading, writing, and math on the elementary level, and individual subjects on the middle and high school levels; also poor study, organizational and/or time-management skills, and teacher-child and/or school-child mismatch.

Psychological or emotional issues: these have their own causes, or may be caused by not addressing the problem issues above.

The issues addressed here will be explored in detail in appropriate sections throughout the book. Chapters 2-7 are organized using **S+T+R+O+N+G**, an acronym for:

> **Self-esteem + Trust + Responsibility +**
> **Options + Needs + Goals**

These are the six areas central to the development of socially and emotionally strong kids. We connect the letters to emphasize that all areas are significant as well as interrelated; thus, none can be left out. Issues of trust hinge on being given responsibility and options; when needs are met, trust develops; when goals are met, self-esteem improves. No one issue can be isolated from another. Many of the case studies here demonstrate that there are often several facets to the problem. But one thing is certain: if parents want their children to succeed in school and life, they need to accept them for who they are, offer support in areas where they can, and keep things in perspective.

Be Patient

Okay, so schools and the school experience are changing — in fact, the whole world is changing. What can you do? This book is teeming with ideas and strategies to help. But have patience! Little problems can be addressed in a short amount of time, but big problems need TIME. If your child is struggling in school — whether due to a deficiency in study skills, a physical disability, an emotional problem, or recent curriculum changes — remember that it will take time to address and correct his difficulties.

Chapter 2

Building Self-esteem

"I hate myself…I'm so stupid."
Jared — Age 14

Jared wore a baseball cap and sat with his head lowered. Mom and Dad sat next to each other with their chairs turned slightly apart. I asked Jared if he knew why he was in my office. "NO," he snapped.

His mother, looking stunned at that answer, quickly responded, "Jared, you're failing everything." Then she turned to me and said, "He keeps calling himself stupid and says he hates himself. I just don't want to hear that type of talk." She turned once again to Jared. "Remember I told you that Dr. Silbert would help you. You just don't listen." Then, when Jared didn't respond, she continued. "Jared, take your hat off. It's not polite to sit with your hat on." She looked at me. "If he'd only come to me for help and stop lying to me about school," she said, followed by a tension-releasing sigh.

To make Jared feel more comfortable and engage him in conversation, I asked him if he was on a junior-varsity sports team, since he was wearing the cap. Still with his head bowed, he mumbled, "No."

In an agitated voice, Dad piped up, "Even that he quit. He was a great player and he won't play anymore. It kills me — and I'm the coach! Now he hangs around with the low-lifes of the school."

Jared had some real issues. First, he needed a little intervention in order to adjust to his parents' recent divorce. Second, he had a rather substantial reading problem. Not only was his comprehension poor, he had difficulty decoding words. When I mentioned this to Mom and Dad, they revealed that Jared had been in remedial reading in elementary school, but they thought he'd outgrown it. I explained to them that since most of his high-school courses involve extensive reading, it was obvious why he was failing.

It was easy to see why Jared felt poorly about himself. His mother's pet expression was, "You can do it," but in reality, he couldn't do it — at least not without the proper support and instruction. To make matters worse, his father appeared to have given up on him. At least that's how Jared perceived it.

Like many children who believe that they cannot live up to their parents' unrealistic expectations, Jared had developed low self-esteem. His symptoms were common: he referred to himself as stupid, said that he hated himself, lied about school, and avoided anything he thought he might not be able to accomplish. Children with low self-esteem often do whatever they can to protect their egos; and at this point, Jared's ego was rather fragile.

Promoting Positive Self-esteem

It takes time, energy, love, and a clear understanding of the components that promote positive self-esteem to raise a strong, self-assured child. If you want to raise a child who is emotionally and socially healthy, then high self-esteem is the key. We cannot overstate its importance. It is an indispensable aspect of human growth and development, in school and out.

But we'd like to make a distinction here between genuine self-esteem and inflated self-esteem.

The Mouse and the Psychiatrist

To overcome his fear of cats, a mouse consulted a mouse psychiatrist. The psychiatrist reassured the mouse, telling him that he was a strong and mighty animal who need not give in to his fear.

The mouse continued his visits, week after week, where he was praised for his strength and ability. After the final session, feeling really good about himself, the mouse departed.

No sooner did he leave, when along came a cat, who...(gulp!) Well, you know what happened.

The moral? *A mouse that is all puffed up is still a mouse.* The psychiatrist did not have to tell the mouse he was a weakling or a coward. However, she should have encouraged him to acquire the skills necessary to avoid a marauding cat. The mouse could then have felt proud of himself for his accomplishments and he would have developed genuine self-esteem. As it was, his ego had been inflated to the point where it distorted his view of himself and the realities of the world he lived in.

The Seven Essential Factors of Self-esteem In Children

1. Knowing their Mom and Dad think they're great! (Chapter 2)
2. Having a safe environment (Chapter 6)
3. Being part of a family, school, and community (Chapter 2)

4. Knowing they are accepted and supported by Mom and Dad (Chapter 2)
5. Being respected by Mom and Dad, and in turn respecting them (Chapter 2)
6. Having logical boundaries (Chapter 4)
7. Having parents with positive self-esteem (Chapter 2)

Supporting and Accepting Your Child for Who He Is

As one of his most important significant others, you, more than anyone else, help to establish how your child feels about himself. There is just no getting around this fact. School personnel, family, and peers have some influence on your child, but yours is the most important. So, how do you help him feel good about himself? By supporting and accepting your child for who he is. Not by putting him down, telling him he isn't strong enough, handsome enough, or smart enough to do something, or discouraging him from doing the things in which he's interested.

Self-esteem Grows Through Your Words and Actions: Let Your Child Know You Think He's Great!

You may not realize how important it is to be aware of how you speak to your child. Are your comments constructive or destructive? What does your face look like when you speak? What does your voice sound like, and what does your body language convey? Your child may perceive messages you don't even know you're sending.

> **When you speak, your child may perceive messages you don't even know you're sending.**

The way your own child thinks you view him—even if you say otherwise, or even if his perceptions are wrong—could be the way he views himself. If children believe that their significant others value them, they are more likely to feel worthy. This factor is critical in their emotional development and school success.

Perceptions are *judgments*. They are highly subjective—based on hunches, opinions, gestures, and other subtle actions. Children can easily misinterpret messages from their significant others; therefore, we need to be sure we don't unwittingly send them unintended messages.

An offhand comment to a friend on the phone that your child hears, for example, ("Oh him, he's just lazy," or "He's driving me nuts") or an exasperated look exchanged between you and your spouse, might say more to your child about your opinion of him than when you say to his face, "I'm so proud of you." You may only be joking with your friend or with your spouse, but your child may pick up on the underlying negative message, even if it's not intended.

If you're proud of your child, don't assume he knows. Express your pride through words and actions.

Siblings, stepparents, grandparents, and other family members also contribute to a child's self-perception to varying degrees. You need to be aware of the opinion they have of your child and how they express it. What are they saying? Are they criticizing your child's conduct or appearance? Does your son ridicule your daughter about her weight or her acne? Does your daughter make fun of your son's poor grades in school? Does Grandma or Grandpa refer to your slow-moving child as "Speedy"? Such comments influence your child's self-esteem and should not be excused as mere teasing.

Be aware of these messages and how your child may perceive them. Then do your best to discourage others from this behavior.

Use Language That Builds Self-esteem

The manner in which you speak to your child will help promote or diminish her self-esteem. Here are some examples of the kinds of phrases that build self-esteem:

- "What a great idea!"
- "That was a good try."
- "I'm proud to be your mom/dad."
- "I always knew you could do it!"
- "I can depend on you."

Think of a time when you were put down, harshly criticized, called names, or cursed at—by your workmates, spouse, children, family or peers. How did you feel? Did you feel like correcting your behavior? Probably not! Chances are, you just felt anger, resentment, and perhaps a negative self-perception.

When your child does something that needs to be corrected, use words that promote growth and esteem. Constructive criticism stresses positive points and suggests improvements. It doesn't cut children down; instead it builds them up.

Negative statements destroy self-esteem. They create ill feelings, confrontations, or stalemates in which your child will cease to try. This typically leads to continuous arguing, avoidance and other anti-social behavior, and needless to say, low self-esteem.

> **When speaking to your child, use constructive
> (not destructive) language.**

Some Negative Statements to Avoid:

- "You're always trying to get away with something."
- "Let's not be stupid."
- "You're such a baby."
- "Your sister would never do such a thing."
- "How are you ever going to amount to anything?"

Similarly, avoid using sarcasm.

- "Okay, genius, you think you can program the video recorder?"
- "Yeah, right. I'm going to let you wear my bracelet to the school dance. You'd lose your head if it weren't attached!"

Think of circumstances in which you may have used such expressions. Did it work? That is, did your child change his behavior because of the criticism? Probably not. Or, if he did change as a result, it may have been out of fear (of your disapproval), not because he understood what he was doing wrong.

> **The bottom line?**
> *Use language that boosts self-esteem.*

Instead of...	Try...
"You're so sloppy! Can't you concentrate more and write your letters neater?	"That looks super! Great colors! Try to print it a little neater and it'll be fantastic."
"You call that a story? It's three sentences long, for crying out loud!"	"Your choice of words is perfect. Let's see if your story has a beginning, a middle, and an end. What do you think?"
"How are you going to get any better at baseball if you don't even try?"	"You did so well at baseball practice, even though I know you're unhappy with your hitting—I saw you throw your bat down. Let's think about what you can do to improve."
"Now why can't you act that way all the time with your sister?"	"I noticed you were sharing with your sister. That feels better than fighting, doesn't it? How did you feel when you shared with her?"
"Stop fighting! You're always fighting!! Can't you just behave with each other for once!!!"	"I heard you fighting with your brother. What do you think you can do to avoid all that yelling and arguing next time?"

Children use us as mirrors. If we think and convey to them that they are wonderful, they will think and believe that they are wonderful. If we think and tell them they are stupid, they will think and believe they are stupid. Our children internalize our words and actions.

The King and His Sons

One rainy day, the king took a walk with his two children. He held an umbrella in each hand to cover and protect each child. A bystander approached and said, "Why are you protecting your children from the rain? You are the king! They should be protecting you."

His highness sagely replied, "If I do not show them respect, how will they learn to respect me? How will they learn to respect others? How will they learn to respect themselves?"

Respect One Another

Respect takes many forms, but the best form is when parent and child respect each other and themselves. Therefore, when your child experiences some trouble in school, before you begin yelling or punishing, think about what you want to teach her.

Michelle — Age 12

Michelle was getting poor grades. Michelle's mom complained that her daughter even curses at her. I asked her if she ever curses at her daughter.

She answered, "Yes, sometimes she makes me so angry."

I told her, "Infant children do not curse at their parents. If they've learned to curse, they picked it up somewhere. If you want her to treat you with respect, you'll have to treat her with respect."

This conversation took place on the telephone. After our first meeting, which centered on school problems, I gave them each an assignment: not to curse at each other that week.

Respect Your Child

When children are treated with respect, they learn to respect themselves and others. So treat your child as you expect to be treated. The ancient tale presented above provides a perfect illustration of the role parents can play when teaching respect. Respect that is genuine, and not simply permissive, promotes self-esteem. It satisfies your child's esteem needs. It makes her feel important—that you hold her in high esteem, and that you value and respect her as a person. There are many ways you can show your child respect.

> **Respect that is genuine, and not simply permissive, promotes self-esteem.**

How to Show Your Child Respect

Do Not Berate

Berating a child models negative behavior; it does not help her to learn, and it shows her total disrespect. For example, a parent who is helping a child to study for a test might make such berating comments as, "We just did this!

What are you, stupid? You're just not paying attention. Now pay attention!" By the end of the session, usually the child is crying and the parent is screaming. And the child may be heard the next day yelling at her classmate, "What are you, stupid?"

A child's forgetfulness often triggers this kind of disrespect from her parents and from other adults. It is common for children to be forgetful. But the same is true for many adults; that's why adults carry laptop computers, daily planners, Palm Pilots® and Blackberries®, and have efficient secretarial personnel to keep them on schedule. In spite of all this assistance, when an adult forgets, we attribute it to a stressful and preoccupied life, yet we can't see the same excuse for children. We forget that *their* lives may be just as stressful to them as our lives are for *us*. So when they slip up once in a while, it's okay. Instead of jumping all over a forgetful child, a more positive and respectful approach is to help her set up methods of support so that she more easily will remember her assignments and responsibilities.

> **Even when correcting or instructing your child, speak with respect.**

Don't Be Sarcastic

Sarcastic remarks are transparent ways of putting someone down, and if directed toward your child, she'll know it. Many parents don't realize that the processes of growth and change take time, and their own frustration causes them to resort to sarcasm. But if you show a lack of respect for your child, she will feel unworthy and less motivated to succeed.

Ask Your Child to Do Grown-up Tasks

There are many opportunities to do so. Asking him to do one at a critical time in his development may be a memorable gift you can give to him. At that moment, he has your respect and trust; he is someone. For example, when the need arises, ask him to answer the phone for you. Even if he forgets to write the person's name next to the number, let him know that you appreciate his help. Next time the situation arises simply remind him to write down both the name and number. This way, he'll learn the same lesson without feeling like a failure.

Control Your Anger

Whether over homework or other issues, many parents become so angry with their children that they end up physically or verbally abusing them. When you get angry at your child, keep this in mind: If you respect someone, do you hit him? Do you curse at him? Do you insult him? Whenever you use physical force or verbal attacks against your child, you show a blatant disregard for his rights and teach him that this is the proper way to express anger and settle disputes. You teach him that it is okay to act on his feelings, when in fact it should be your goal to teach him to think first, and think clearly, before he acts.

The bottom line: Give your children the kind of respect you expect from them.

Be Sure Your Child Is Being Treated Respectfully At School

Not only is it important for you to treat your child with respect; it is also important to be sure that your child is being treated respectfully at school. The following is an excerpt from an open letter from a student I taught to read years ago.

"I have dyslexia. That doesn't make me stupid!"
Maria — Age 25

I have dyslexia. I've had it all my life. That made learning to read very difficult for me. When I was in school I was so frustrated with anything involving reading that I wanted to scream. In fact, my dyslexia made school a living hell.

Teachers would give me work and say, "Do the best you can." Duh, I couldn't even read the directions on the top of the sheet, so I just sat there not knowing what to do. All they kept saying was, "Maria, do your work!"

One day when I was trying to read a sentence, one of the kids said out loud, "That's the same word you just read. What are you, stupid?" And, you guessed it, the whole class heard it and laughed at me. I ran out of the room so they wouldn't see me crying.

It was a long hard road, but I learned how to compensate — to overcome my dyslexia — so now I am able to read just about as well as normal readers. What took me even longer to learn is that I am all right, that I am not stupid.

In fact, I finished college and earned a masters degree in special education. I am now a special education teacher, and I enjoy helping students who have learning disabilities.

Thanks to brain research, the dyslexia dark ages is rapidly coming to a close. Teachers and other reading specialists now know that dyslexia is not reading backwards; it is a learning disability centered in the language portion of the brain. With appropriate intervention, dyslexia can be overcome.

I am also writing this secretly wishing it were possible to deliver the message to all kids who have dyslexia or any other type of learning disability. They need to know that they are not alone, that they can believe in themselves, and even more importantly, that they are not stupid.

As a student, Maria was not alone. There are countless Marias who struggle with dyslexia and/or other learning disabilities. Due to their disabilities, these children are often misunderstood. And, even worse, they are not treated with the respect they deserve. I have had numerous learning-disabled children tell me that their teachers write assignments on the board and then tell the class to do the assignment. This may work for students who are able to read, but it doesn't work for those who can't.

One tenth-grader told me that he puts his head on his desk and pretends he is sleeping because he is too embarrassed to tell the teacher that he cannot read the assignment on the board. When I spoke to the teacher she dismissed him as a discipline problem because he "refuses to do the work." I informed her that he couldn't read it and was too embarrassed to tell her in fear of her reaction or the other students' reactions. The teacher was shocked; she had no idea that his reading ability was so limited. She and the student were then able to come up with something that worked.

As your child's number-one advocate, be sure she is treated respectfully, both at home and at school. For the most part, teachers and other school personnel are wonderful, hard-working people who care about education and children. But sometimes they too need to be informed. If you see that your child is not being treated with the respect she deserves, call her teacher. Chances are he or she is unaware of your child's problem and will appreciate your call.

As for Maria, while it took a long time and a lot of hard work on her part, she learned how to compensate. And now she is a popular and successful special education teacher.

Help Your Children Grow Their Own Way

What areas of his education, social life, or home life does your child value most? Are they different from those that you value?

Were you an accounting major in college? Your child might like history. Do you treasure the arts? She may prefer sports. Do you take her to baseball games? She may prefer tennis.

> **Self-esteem is built when your child develops in areas *she* considers valuable, not in those that *you* decide should be valuable.**

So provide your child with room to grow, and allow her latitude for individual action. This is important for all children, but especially for creative types. Often such youngsters do not seem to fit comfortably into the tidy arrangements of our lives or of a school's curriculum. However, in many cases, these are the very children who, given the opportunity, often come up with genuinely innovative ideas. If you read the biographies of the most creative people in business, entertainment, arts and sciences — people like Thomas Edison and Albert Einstein — you will learn that they did not fit into the academic system very well. Yet they all succeeded in life — and then some!

Lynnette — Age 9

Lynnette and her mother came to our office because her mother felt that Lynnette had low self-esteem. Like Jared, Lynette described herself as stupid and said she hated school.

Lynnette was doing poorly in school. Her mother sat for hours each day helping her with her homework. When asked if she enjoyed sitting with her mother, Lynette said, "No, I hate it." Her mother was frustrated with Lynette because she felt that her daughter wasn't trying. With that, Lynnette rolled her eyes and called her mother "a pain."

During our conversations, Lynette revealed that she loved to dance, but that her mother had withdrawn her from dancing class so that Lynnette could study more.

After testing Lynnette, I diagnosed her as having a learning disability. She had difficulty processing language; therefore, school was indeed difficult for her. It was taking Lynnette much longer to process information than the other children in her class. That is also why she still did not succeed even after her mother lectured her for hours. At this point, the school did further testing. We arranged to have a tutor go to her home one hour each week, and the school arranged for her to receive some additional support during the day.

I told Mom that in order to establish a more positive relationship with her daughter, and to help her daughter grow intellectually and emotionally, she would need to focus on areas other than school. School obviously is very important, but her daughter needed space to be herself, and to shine in one or more activities that interested her.

With her mother's encouragement, Lynnette chose to go back to dancing school. This gave Lynette the opportunity to create, evaluate, plan, and organize outside of school. As she succeeded, she began to feel better about herself. As she felt better about herself, her schoolwork dramatically improved. This was not a coincidence. Lynnette had learned important skills at dance that she could apply at school. The combination of success at dance and improvement at school boosted her self-esteem.

Encourage Your Child's Development

Through your words and actions, there are many ways you can encourage your child's development. Here are some ways to get started.

Respect Your Child's Inherited Physical Endowments

Nobody, thank goodness, is physically perfect. So encourage your child to accept his or her physical appearance. Children are acutely self-conscious about their physical selves — a girl might be embarrassed by her large nose, a boy about his pimples. Your child might even hate the very qualities you find adorable — his big ears, or her curly hair — so convey your acceptance of his or her physical endowments.

You might be quite proud of your child just the way he is. But does your child know this? He needs to, even when nothing out of the ordinary is happening. Remind him every day that you support him, and show him the same through your actions.

Be Open and Available

Are you approachable? When you are working at home, watching television, or doing housework, is your body language telling your child that you don't want to be bothered? Or are you showing her that you will listen if she has a problem?

Does your child see you as someone she can ask for help?

Of course, there are times when you are doing something important or taking care of your own needs. You can't be accessible twenty-four hours a day, and you don't have to be a problem-solver all the time, but you do need to be someone your child can count on to talk to when the need arises. It will help her just to know you're there, ready to listen and not judge. If a child perceives that a parent is too busy, disinterested, or annoyed to hear her, then her problems, no matter how trivial they may seem to adults, may overwhelm her.

Recognize and Applaud Effort

Did your child bungle an art project? Miss a ground ball in a baseball game? Spill a mixing bowl while trying to make cake batter? You know that the effort he puts into the activity is far more important than the success or failure of it, but he probably doesn't know that. So tell him! Even better than saying, "That's okay, it's the effort that counts," would be to say, "I'm proud of you for trying to make a cake; most kids your age would never tackle that. And you got the ingredients just right!" or "I can see that you threw away the art project you started. I'm sorry you didn't like it. But I'm proud that you took on such a difficult task."

Be Receptive and Helpful With Your Child's Personal Problems – Seek Help From Professionals When Appropriate

It takes only a few minutes each day to ask how your child feels and then listen attentively to what he or she says. Instead of asking general questions about school activities, for example, you could try drawing out your child to see if there are any personal problems you are unaware of. So, for example, instead of asking, "How was school today?" you might ask, "Was school better today? Yesterday you said that your teacher kept you in during recess. Did you go out today?" If the answer is yes or no, try to ask more leading questions, such as "What changed today that made things better (or worse)?" and then continue from there. Or, instead of asking, "Did you do your homework?" try asking something like "You said last week that you had a history report due. How is it coming?" If it seems that things are not going well, you may want to offer help or suggest some alternative strategies such as after-school assistance or private tutoring.

"I wonder which strategy Gilford uses to remember to clean his room...May be time for a new strategy."

You might also try to be more attuned to your child's moods—to detect, for example, signs of depression. Take the time to find out why he may be troubled. And, if something serious arises, don't shoulder the entire burden yourself. You would not hesitate to go to a physician if your child were physically ill; seek help from a mental health professional when he seems psychologically troubled or is behaving unusually. The school counselor, social worker and psychologist are great resources.

Offer Opportunities to Pursue Individual Interests

Your child can't find areas to explore her individuality if she is not exposed to different activities. When notices for clubs or sports leagues are posted or handed out in school, encourage your child to enroll if she shows an interest. And get her presents that suit her interests. If she is interested in building, why buy her dolls? Children are often scared to try new things. By encouraging (but not forcing) them to try out new activities, we can help them discover areas in which they may express their individuality.

Encourage Your Child to Evaluate the Opinions and Values of Others Instead of Submissively Adopting Them

It's a sign of low self-esteem when a child accepts without question other people's ideas and values. Encourage your child to weigh each situation instead of mindlessly going along with the decisions or opinions of others. At the same time, encourage him to seek support for his own ideas. This way, your child will learn to determine whether or not a value or opinion is of worth to him, and thereby gain power over his own decisions. This will help his self-esteem as a child, and will serve him well when he is older, when more potentially damaging ideas (such as drug use, sex, or prejudice, for example) will be presented to him.

> **It's a sign of low self-esteem when a child accepts without question other kids' opinions and values.**

Initiate Activities That Involve Creating and Doing

Working on a creative level stimulates one of the highest forms of intellectual growth. By creating and carrying out projects on their own, children plan, organize, cooperate, and evaluate. These things may not seem important when you're trying to get dinner on the table, bathe the kids, or get them to finish their homework, but they are. They are the very skills needed to succeed in school, and in life.

Be a Good Role Model

Children have a better chance of developing high self-esteem when those closest to them, primarily their parents, demonstrate high self-esteem. After all, children learn from modeled behavior.

What you *do* influences your child's character far more than what you *say*. If you have high self-esteem and exude confidence, you pass those traits on to your children by example. If, on the other hand, you are unhappy with your job, don't have the courage to talk to your boss, and are depressed or self-deprecating, your child is not being brought up in an emotional climate conducive to developing high self-esteem. Obviously, these emotional by–products of a stressful life can be dealt with, and it is important that you, as a parent, learn how to—so your child can grow from your example and learn how to deal with life's curveballs.

*Suggestions for promoting **your** self-esteem*

- **Share your original ideas, opinions, and thoughts with peers and family members.** Don't just take on the ideas and opinions of others.
- **Take action; don't just talk.** Show your child that you are a doer, not just a talker.
- **Respond to feedback.** Don't automatically consider what others say to be more important than what you have to say.
- **Set realistic short- and long-term goals for yourself.** What do you hope to accomplish this year? In ten years? What kind of person would you like to be?
- **Attend to your personal needs:** eat well, get plenty of sleep, exercise, and be sure to leave some time for fun.

- **Sort out your options so that you can make appropriate decisions.** Recognize that you have the capacity to help determine your destiny and not let others determine it for you.
- **Establish a realistic idealized image for yourself and work toward it.**
- **Work toward becoming competent in one or more areas in which you aspire.** Be sure your goals are realistic.

> **Show your child that you are a doer, not just a talker.**

Self-esteem Grows When Kids Feel That They Are Part of a Family, School, and Community

Mary Beth — Age 9

"I'm so excited! Sunday is my birthday. So Mommy and Daddy are taking me to the mall Saturday and we're going to eat there and then go to the movies. Jessica and Amanda are going, too. They're my two best friends. Steven is taking a friend, too, because otherwise he'd bother us. Then Sunday, Grandma Angela, Grandpa Peter, Grandma Pearl and Papa, Aunt Theresa and Uncle Joe, Aunt Susan, and all my cousins are coming over for dinner. We're gonna have a barbecue and ice cream cake. Then, on Monday, Mommy's gonna bring cupcakes to my class. I just can't wait!"

Mary Beth was a fourth grader who clearly had some physical disabilities and learning disabilities that required her to work harder than most of her classmates in order to learn new material, catch a ball, or ride a bike. Yet, she didn't seem to have any emotional problems as a result of her disabilities. In fact, she was quite proud of who she was.

Mary Beth was fortunate to have parents who were not only loving, but extremely supportive. In addition, she had the luxury of a supportive extended family. She was an integral part of her family, which helped her get through her school and social experiences with fewer scars than would a child whose need to belong was not being met at home. On the occasions when she did well in school, she shared her excitement not only with Mommy and Daddy, but also with Grandma Angela, Grandpa Peter, Grandma Pearl and Papa. When she went on a class trip, Aunt Theresa traded stories with her about her own trip to the same place. Because he was a math teacher, Uncle Joe helped her with her math homework. Because her parents worked every other weekend, Aunt Susan took Mary Beth and her cousins to the library on Saturdays. If she succeeded, they were there to celebrate with her. If she failed, they were there to console and support her. And she was there for them. When Papa had an operation, she called him and read him stories over the phone. Mary Beth was a lucky child, a full-fledged member of a loving and supporting family.

Belonging to the Family

Belonging to a family is an important factor in a child's development, whether he is an only child or one of eight. But even an only child may feel left out of decision-making and other family dynamics. He might be in day care during the mornings, with a babysitter in the afternoons, rushed through dinner in the evening and put to bed at night, without ever getting the sense that he is an important part of the family. In effect, his family might be happening around him. When he becomes a teenager, this child may be a "loner," or may turn to his peers for acceptance and love, because at home he has never felt this critical sense of belonging.

> **Be careful that your child doesn't feel that his family is happening around him.**

Suggestions for helping your child feel a sense of belonging in your family

- **Work — and play — together.** Some chores provide a great opportunity to involve your child. If you make the experience a pleasant one, and he knows that he will be able to take play breaks, he may enjoy the experience and prove to be a good helper. Then, after the chores are done, consider a fun activity together.
- **Build a sense of familial pride by supporting one another.** Allow your child to be your cheerleader once in a while to show her that you are strengthened by her support — when, for example, you are taking on an important project at work or beginning a new exercise program. Moreover, let her know as well that her sibling(s) needs her support and encouragement too. She will feel more important as a result.
- **Encourage all family members to be proud of themselves.** Show your child that you support what makes each family member unique, and that each person makes a valuable contribution to the family in his or her own way. One parent might not have

a regular out-of-the-house job, but is contributing emotionally and educationally, if not financially, to the family. A child might be tone-deaf but has a wonderful sense of humor. Each one should know that the others are valued for what he or she brings to the family unit.

- **Teach your child how to be a group member.** Being members of groups does not come naturally to most children; it is not easy for them to compromise their personal desires for the general good. As a member of one group — your family — your child needs to learn to follow the rules established by and for the group.

- **Encourage your child to help others.** Maybe your child can help the three-year-old girl next door to tie her shoes. Or, when a disabled person is having difficulty getting through the front door of a store, perhaps you can ask your child to hold it open. (Note: Be sure not to push this point. If you insist on nagging your child about this, he may end up resenting it and thinking you care more about others than you do for him.)

- **Plan a party or do something special for another member of the family.** Kids love to be included in the planning of a special event. Your child could help you make breakfast-in-bed for someone, then carry it in himself; he can plan a birthday party for his brother or sister, right down to mailing the invitations, shopping for snacks, and baking the cake; or he can surprise family members by cleaning their rooms for them or by making their lunches.

Belonging to the School Community

As she gets older, your child needs to feel that she belongs not only to her family, but also to other groups she joins. School introduces her to an important new community; she will need to feel a sense of belonging there. School personnel will work to foster a sense of community at your child's school, but you can help as well.

"I hate the kids in my school...I can't wait to get out of here. Why can't we move back?"

Paula — Age 15

It was January when I first met Paula King, a tenth grader. Her family had moved from the Midwest to the suburbs of New York City. Her father had been transferred and her mom was able to find a job locally. Mrs. King said that the move was difficult for all of them because they left behind family and friends. "But sometimes you don't have a choice," she said as she turned to Paula.

"We investigated all the towns around New York City and found this one to match our needs," interjected Dad.

"Well, I hate it," chimed in Paula.

As the session went on, I learned that Paula had received A's and B's in her old school, but now she was receiving C's and failing two courses.

It was easy to see that Paula was having difficulty becoming part of her new school. She felt like the outsider looking in — and, in fact, she was. Her roots were far away, and now she needed to plant new ones so that she'd become a part of her new school community. Paula was experiencing what all children and teens go through when they move or change schools. She needed to become part of her new environment.

Like Paula, many children do not feel as if they are part of their school community, which makes learning that much more difficult. They are so uncomfortable, and feel so poorly about themselves in that setting, that they have difficulty concentrating, seeking help, joining clubs, and attending after-school events. To experience this, a child doesn't have to move from one state or town to another; this could be the case as well when a child transfers from public school to private school, or from private school to public school. As one recently transplanted sixteen-year-old told me, "I always feel as if everyone is wearing black shoes and I'm wearing brown."

When I contacted Paula's guidance counselor, we struck gold. The counselor became her safety net at school, got her teachers on board, and helped to get her involved in the school chorus, the science club and the after-school dance. Soon Paula was connected. She made some good friends and became more comfortable in the school setting. Paula was clearly becoming part of her school community; she felt a sense of belonging. As a result, her grades began to improve.

Paula's parents played an important role in Paula's turn-around; they recognized that their daughter was having difficulty, and they helped her become a part of her new school's community.

It will also help if you are involved as a parent because when your child shares what goes on at school, you'll be able to relate. So communicate with teachers often, volunteer at school events, attend PTA and school board meetings and request programs and services if you need them.

Belonging to the Local Community

Your child will benefit from participating in his extended neighborhood or community. This may be easier said than done as your life may be so hectic that you may not feel much like a member of your own community yourself. Regardless, there are many things you can do to help your child feel a sense of belonging to the town where you live — his hometown.

Eric — Age 17

Eric was perhaps the most learning-disabled child I had ever worked with. His parents and other family members thought he was great, and so did his teachers. But as he got older, he began to think that his peers thought he was dumb. As his peers were now increasingly important significant others in his life, his perception that they thought poorly of him caused his self-esteem to plummet. He began to hate school. His parents' and teachers' attempts to help him feel good about himself were fruitless.

This all changed when he turned sixteen and was able to join the volunteer fire department. His competence in this endeavor gave him a feeling of importance that he had not known before. He knew then that he had the respect not only of his peers, but of the other adults in the community.

Suggestions for helping your child feel as though she is a part of the local community:

- Encourage your child to play with the neighborhood kids and to join a youth group, team, or club.
- Take your child to the public library — not just for books, but for activities as well.
- Have your child volunteer at a local hospital, historical society, or religious or other community institution.

- Show your child his community's special features and resources—its buildings, parks, natural features, stores, and schools.
- Set a good example for your child by participating in community events.
- Instruct your child on what to say and do in social situations, such as talking to an elderly person who has difficulty hearing, attending a funeral, or just some pointers on chatting with neighbors at the community gathering. Naturally, these events have to be age appropriate.

Chapter 3

Creating Trust

"I don't trust anybody. Why should I?"
Lucy — Age 16

The first time Lucy came to my office, her mom and dad had to physically nudge her through the door. I stood up and met her halfway. "Hi," I said, "I bet you don't want to be here, do you?"

"I don't care," snapped Lucy. "Whatever."

I told Lucy that I didn't blame her. It was a beautiful Saturday afternoon, and I wouldn't have wanted to be there either if I had been in her shoes. Her face loosened up a little bit and she seemed to relax. I told her that we would meet only for one hour, and then afterwards she could do as she pleased.

"You must be kidding!" she snapped again, then looked at her mom. "Like she's going to let me go to the mall with my friends."

I assured her that I didn't care if she got 100's or zeroes because I didn't have a refrigerator with fruit-shaped magnets on which to post her grades. She smiled a little. I told her that my only job was to help her learn how to learn, so she could get out of high school and go onto the career of her choice. I also told her that while she was working with me, her parents were not allowed to ground her or punish her over school issues. At this she smiled again and came all the way into my office with her parents.

After speaking with the three of them for a while, I learned that Mom wanted her to go to a top-notch college, so Lucy had to get top-notch grades. Her stepdad went along with whatever Mom wanted, even though he felt that she was a little too severe at times. Her dad was cool, she said, but she wasn't with him that often — just every other weekend.

Lucy talked about how her parents punished her when she got poor grades. "I wasn't even allowed to go to the Winter Ball in tenth grade because I didn't make high honors."

"If you're struggling in school, whom do you turn to?" I asked Lucy.

"Not her for sure," she said, looking over at Mom. "She'd only ground me. That's so dumb, like grounding me is going to make me understand English or math. She doesn't get it."

"So, you don't go to Mom because you don't feel safe going to her?" She nodded. "Then why don't you go to your stepdad? You said he's not as strict?"

"No, he feels sorry for me, but I can't trust him. He always goes to my mom after I talk to him."

"What about your dad?" I asked. "You're with him every other weekend, and you just told me that you call him all the time, and he's real cool."

"Yeah, but I can't count on him to help me. He says he will, but he never does. I don't trust anyone!"

At this, Mom interrupted. "Lucy," she said, "it goes two ways. You say you don't trust us. Well, we don't trust you! You always tell me that you're doing fine and then I find out that you failed some test or didn't hand something in. That's why I ground you — because you lie to me. Not because you're having problems at school!"

"I wouldn't lie to you if I knew you wouldn't go ballistic every time I got even an 80," Lucy said. "You always say

that you're here to help me, but all you do is go behind my back, you know, like calling my teachers. They tell you some lie — like I keep talking in class or even fall asleep sometimes — and then you end up yelling at me and taking away my social life. You call that helping?"

Mom continued, "Lucy, I only called Mrs. Green because she called me. You were downright rude to her...no less falling asleep everyday in her class!"

"You should have come to me first before you called her...But no...You wouldn't believe me anyway."

Trust was apparently a problem in this family. Even though Mom said she wanted what was best for Lucy, she was actually harming her daughter and their relationship by being so focused on Lucy's grades and not talking things over with her before calling the school. She had forgotten the importance of role modeling and the need to respect and trust her daughter. Mom said that she understood the need to be calm and helpful, but when she saw Lucy's grades, she would invariably act on her emotions. Her stepfather would side with Lucy so that Lucy felt she had someone to turn to, but then he would betray her trust by telling Mom everything. Lucy's only hope was her dad, but by making promises he rarely kept, he too had shown that he could not be trusted.

What did Lucy learn from a home environment that was not worthy of trust? *She learned to lie and do anything she could to avoid punishment.*

What children learn at home often manages to find its way outside the home.

I asked Lucy if she trusted her teachers. Again she responded with a resounding "NO!" I asked her to give me specific examples of what they had done that had earned her distrust. "If I talk to my friend for a second, they say I'm always talking. Or like I fell asleep in Mrs. Green's class once or twice...big deal!"

I asked Lucy how she would feel if she invited twenty-five kids to her house for a Saturday night party. The night of the party, most of the kids arrived late. Some were defiant and didn't go along with any of the planned activities; for example, they continued talking while she was telling a really great joke. One ignored the party altogether and sat in a corner and went to sleep. How would she feel?

Lucy quietly answered, "Pretty lousy."

Then I asked her to visualize what it was like teaching twenty-five kids at the same time, hour after hour, day after day. That's what teachers do, I told her. Every day they plan what they hope would be a pleasant lesson — sort of like a party — and they feel pretty upset, and sometimes downright angry, when some kids in the class ruin everything by being uncooperative, defiant or rude, or even by going to sleep. This anecdote helped Lucy get the point.

I have shared this example with many kids so that they could understand that teachers are people too. And if they treated their teachers with respect and trust, then their teachers would in turn treat them with respect and trust.

Being Trusting and Being Trustworthy

You have to trust your child and he has to trust you. From infancy on, children need to learn to trust others. Starting with their significant others, they learn to trust that their earliest cries of hunger and discomfort will bring relief. In a protective and nurturing home environment, the number of trusting relationships branch out from there.

The other dimension of trust, trustworthiness, develops later. It has to be learned. One of the best ways of imbuing trustworthiness in children is by example. Do your best to be a trustworthy person for your child while also showing that you trust her. This will greatly increase the likelihood that she will grow up to be a trustworthy and trusting adult.

As for Lucy, things gradually improved. Each week she and Mom were asked to select one example of how they didn't trust each other. They kept a journal noting what happened and how they responded to each other. During the first week Lucy promised to tell her Mom about any poor grade. Her Mom promised that she would stay calm and focus on the cause of the poor grade and see how she could be of assistance. She agreed that she would not use punishment as the solution. When they came in the next week they both brought in their journals. They were empty. They laughed that neither of them remembered to fill it in. I told them I appreciated that they were honest about the journal; I could trust them to tell me the truth. Lucy began by telling me that she had failed a math test, and her mom said that when it happened, she controlled her first instinct to ground her; instead they talked about what happened. They realized together that Lucy simply didn't understand the topic, even after going to the teacher for extra help. They hired a tutor to help her with this math topic.

We met weekly for about a year. Lucy and her mom started sharing more and more. Lucy's grades fluctuated, so we talked about the reasons for each grade, whether they were A's, B's or C's. I introduced many strategies that helped her learn how to learn. That year her grades continued to improve. As for Lucy's mom, she changed jobs and began to put a great deal of energy into her work. This helped her transfer her goals away from Lucy. She was still there to talk to her, but she stopped obsessing over her grades. Her step-dad agreed that the fighting at home between Lucy and her Mom had gone from an everyday occurrence to a rare one. Lucy's dad promised that he would follow through when Lucy went to him with a problem. She later reported that he had begun to keep his promises. Lucy now had a safer environment because she could trust the most significant others in her life.

Improving family relationships that are deficient in trust is hard work for everyone involved and it takes time. Sometimes it is not this simple because one or more of the people involved find change too difficult. If this happens, the family would do well to consider family therapy.

How to Promote Both Dimensions of Trust In Children

Show your child that you are an ally, physically as well as emotionally.

Some parents are good at showing up, but not at helping their children's emotional needs. Others are good at soothing, listening to, and caring for the emotional needs of their children, but can not be counted on to be there at a predetermined time and place when their children expect them. Your child needs to trust that you will be there for him in both situations. When he and you have an appointment to meet somewhere, it will reassure him to see you there. Your emotional presence when he is sad, lonely, or hurt is equally important; it will comfort him to be able to talk to you about his problems.

Be consistent so that your child can anticipate your behavior.

If you behave unpredictably, your child will learn to be wary of you instead of trusting in you. Don't, for example, promise to help your child build a playhouse over the weekend if you know your have other commitments. Don't help him with his guitar lessons one day, only to brush him off the next three times. Also, if possible, make every effort to come home from work at about the same time every day, especially when the children are young. If this is not possible, try to keep your children in the loop so they'll at least know what to expect.

Keep promises, agreements, and secrets.

If your child confides in you that she has trouble in biology and you get her a tutor, and you agree to keep this confidential because she is embarrassed about it, then you cannot share this with your brother Frank at the Memorial Day cookout when he asks about her. Would you then blame her if she thought twice about trusting you again with such confidential information?

Tell and show your child that you trust her.

Demonstrate your trust by asking her to carry a grocery bag, or by entrusting her with a possession you value (a pair of costume earrings, a pet, a book) — and don't get all bent out of shape if she loses or breaks it! If she does not have the trust of her most significant others, she may begin to believe herself unworthy of trust. Use your judgment to match the responsibility to your child's age and maturation level.

By the end of the third quarter of her junior year, Lucy and her mom came to my office again for a follow up.

Although Lucy's grades were still lackluster in math and English, Mom did not overreact. When Lucy asked if she could get some tutoring to help her prepare for the math final, Mom agreed. And since Mom had been an English major in college, she suggested that she be the one to help Lucy prepare for the English final. Lucy cheerfully agreed.

In the interim since our first visit, Lucy had seen that Mom had changed and that she could now count on her to keep her promises. In turn, Lucy showed her mom that she, too, could be trusted.

On Lying

Let's digress a little to discuss a big school-related issue: lying. Lying is a common strategy children use to conceal from their parents problems they are having in school. To them, the consequences of getting caught in a lie will be less severe than the verbal or physical abuse they know they'll face if they tell the truth about their troubles. The abuse extends beyond shouting and punishment. To many children, recopying an entire paper just because it is too messy is torture, as is correcting twenty of their math problems or looking up thirty misspelled words. For them, the risks associated with lying may be worth taking. If the worst-case scenario happens and they are caught, at least the focus changes from school issues to lying issues, territory that has more predictable consequences. Think about it: generally speaking, isn't it an unfortunate state of family disharmony when lying feels safer to children than confiding in their parents?

Be someone your child can trust, someone safe to talk to

One way to do this is to talk to your child every day about school, even if it's just for a few minutes. Sometimes, of course, she will give monosyllabic answers to your questions and not appear at all willing to share. This may be because she perceives that you are interrogating her, or because it's simply not a good time.

If there never seems to be time to work in a talk, the best time to have a discussion may be at the dinner table, when she is a captive audience. Having a meal together, at least once a day, presents the perfect opportunity to discover what is really going on at school. Most parents remember to check homework, but attention should also be given to the work your child does in the classroom. This does not mean to interrogate, ridicule, or punish her for poor work. Instead, this should be an opportunity to establish a trusting relationship and get a greater sense of your child's interests and concerns regarding school.

> *Sally:* "Oh, did I mess up on my biology test! You know, the circulation system questions."
>
> *Dad:* "I think I messed up on that, too, when I took Bio years ago."
>
> *Mom:* "I had trouble with that too. What helped me was using one of those mnemonic devices. Later, I'll show you what I used. I think it will help you."
>
> *Sally:* "Good. I'll need it. I'm calling Cindy to see how she did."

Sally had a strong, healthy relationship with her parents. She trusted that she would be safe from verbal abuse if she told them that she messed up. They were on the same team working toward the same goal. Conversations like these will increase the likelihood of family relationships based on trust—and, of course, from trust comes honesty.

> **Let your child know from the very first day of school that he, his parents and teacher are all on the same team. If he needs help, he'll get it.**

Homework and Trust

As homework often takes center stage when it comes to children lying to parents, let us continue the digression to explore the relationship between homework and trust.

Amy—Age 14

Amy came to us at two different stages in her development. First, when she was in second grade, her parents were concerned that she was not being sufficiently challenged in school. They brought her to me for an evaluation. Amy was adorable; it was easy to see why her loving, well-meaning parents, worshipped their only child. The testing went smoothly.

During the follow-up session, I remember telling Mom and Dad to appreciate who they have; that Amy was an adorable, bright little girl, and they need not hover over her. I assured them that she would be just fine.

But that was then. Somehow, over the years, the relationship had changed, and so did Amy. I got to see her again seven years later. In that time she had become an angry teenager who was failing two subjects. Her mother brought her to me because she was exasperated over her inability to get Amy to do her homework.

Once her mom left us alone, Amy's demeanor began to soften, and pretty soon she opened up. She told me that her mom was right; she didn't get her homework done, because what she didn't finish at school or during the bus ride simply went undone. Why? Remember the hovering from seven years earlier? Now a teenager yearning for independence, she could no longer tolerate Mom or Dad scrutinizing every word—spelling, punctuation, grammar, dictionaries, thesauruses, recopying—and she was ready to flip out.

Her solution? In classic, teenage-brain-logic fashion: never again allow them to see her homework. If it didn't get done in school or during the bus ride, it didn't exist. Once home, the lying and cover-ups began: "Nope, no homework." or "Got it all done in school...honest!" Needless to say, she missed numerous homework assignments!

Homework can be one of the most frustrating of all problem areas for children and parents—a source of

"Try to get the bus driver to slow down.
I'm not done with my homework yet."

much family discord. Parents find themselves facing a full spectrum of choices when it comes to dealing with such issues, the extremes being authoritative on one end and permissive on the other end. As a parent, it is wise to beware of the consequences of taking the extreme positions. Keeping school in perspective requires that you monitor continuously the child-parent-teacher-homework situation.

Avoid books whose titles are some variations of *THIS IS THE ONLY WAY TO GET YOUR CHILD TO DO HOME-WORK*. And don't blindly accept THE ONLY WAY from your best friend Blanche, the educational philosopher. That is not to say that those approaches are no good; it's just that either one may be a terrible mismatch for your child. Instead, make the effort to identify the real cause of the homework issue, and attempt to resolve it. While not necessarily easy to do, it is well worth the effort because when you succeed, the issue of lying/lack of trust will likely cease to be a problem.

The Real Causes Behind Homework Issues

1. The homework is too difficult.

If the homework is continuously too difficult, with everything that entails, then a child will try to avoid it. Look into the cause. Begin by having a conversation with the teacher. If the problem is class-wide, hopefully the teacher will evaluate and adjust the nature of his or her homework assignments. If the problem is limited to your child, she may require additional help from the teacher after school, from you, from a sibling, from a teenager you hire, or from a tutor. If this fails to resolve the issue, then a reevaluation of the type of class, or course level, or teaching vs. learning style, or school may be in order.

On the other hand, the cause of the problem may be a disability: physical, learning and/or attentional. Examples include: *hearing, seeing, reading, language processing, writing,* and *ADHD (or ADD)*. If the problem is one of these, sometimes it is easy to resolve.

Let's examine one disability, dysgraphia, which makes writing very difficult. In addition to making writing assignments painful, it affects *all* areas peripherally. For example, since keeping numbers lined up in columns is difficult, math computations are fertile grounds for disaster. Also, think about how much trouble it must be for these children to copy an assignment from the board and then decrypt it once home. The following illustrates just how exasperating dysgraphia must have been for this otherwise normal, bright young child.

Baldwin Age—11

Baldwin had severe dysgraphia, but for some reason it had not been diagnosed by the school. By the time I met him, he was a sixth grader and was failing almost everything. Hardened by the sum total of his experiences, on test papers that required writing he had recently begun to write the following on otherwise blank papers: "I'd rather get a '0' than take your stupid test."

Hard to believe, isn't it? The zero he could deal with—the writing he could not. Did he do his homework? No. Would the issue have been resolved by continuing authoritative rules and harsh punishments? No. In fact, he did not begin his academic turnaround until he was classified with dysgraphia. It was then that he began receiving the support he needed to help him compensate so he was able to succeed—in fact, *excel*—in school. This support involved Baldwin's learning keyboarding, being allowed to use a laptop computer in place of handwriting in school, having the assistance of a scribe in certain settings, and having class notes and assignments written or photocopied for him.

2. The homework is too confusing.

When children chronically complain that assignments or directions are confusing, they are likely to become frustrated and/or anxious, eventually avoiding such assignments. Parents usually respond to these children by asking, "Weren't you listening? Or "Just read the directions!" They *were* listening or reading, but they may not have been able to process the information.

In this case, the cause may be reading comprehension and/or language processing problems. Parents should seek the help of teachers or a learning specialist to help a child learn strategies she can use to overcome or compensate for the disability.

If neither of these areas are the cause of the problem, then parents need to investigate why their child continues to complain. If it turns out it is simply a ploy to get the parents to do the work with—or for—them, then the issue changes and the reason for the behavior needs to be addressed. In some cases, the child simply wants the company of a parent during homework time. Wow! How's that for the ultimate compliment?

3. The homework is too low-quality or too boring.

Sometimes homework assignments are low-quality boring busywork and children will avoid them simply because they don't want to do them. Unfortunately, one of life's little lessons that children need to learn is that sometimes we simply have to do boring things—and they have to do the work. If, however, every assignment appears to be dull, too easy, or too low-quality, the parent needs to talk to the teacher to determine the purpose of the assignments. Many teachers do not realize how some of the assignments are coming across to the children; chances are they will appreciate the feedback and adjust the work as appropriate.

4. The child is disorganized.

He brings home the book and forgets the assignment. He brings home the assignment and forgets the book. Or both. Does this describe your child? If so, it sounds like you've got yourself a disorganized child. The same is true for children who can't judge time or can't manage their time. They may have the best intentions to get the homework done, but somehow it gets lost in their time-maze.

It is so difficult for disorganized children to get their homework done that some of them would rather lie, insisting that there is no homework, than be criticized and punished. (See pp. 123-127 for some suggestions on how to help your child become more organized.)

5. The homework is too intrusive.

It's a fact; homework cuts into playtime. So what's the problem? The problem is that in some cases homework time creeps up to the point of consuming the home lives of the children and sometimes that of the family as well. Besides the obvious down side, this may be harmful to children's intellectual development. Their brains are developing and they need to use all parts, and good quality play provides opportunities to use the "far corners" of the brain that might otherwise remain fallow. So, it turns out that children *need* to play. Surprisingly, brain research indicates that occasional boredom is good, too, as it forces children to think of things to do — that is, to use their brains to create.

So if homework time seems to have taken over your home, work out a schedule with your child so that he doesn't have to lie in order to play.

53

6. Too much parent involvement.

Some parents are simply overly involved in their child's homework. Here are the three most common types, all of whom tend to drive their children toward lying and deception. If any of these describe you, then work to change your behavior.

A. **The "perfectionist parents."** Perfectionists demand picture-perfect-homework. Their children hate to let them see their homework papers out of fear that they will judge the work unworthy, tear it up, and make them do it again. Besides being tedious and time demanding, in these extreme cases, it is downright disrespectful of the child.

B. **The "helicopter parents."** These parents, like Amy's, hover over their children, making sure that every "t" is crossed and every "i" is dotted. By not giving their children any breathing room, they are delivering the tacit message that their children are not capable of doing the work themselves. Not only does this harm their self-esteem, it denies their children the opportunity of taking responsibility for their own work.

C. **The "Pandora parents."** The children of Pandora parents tend to deny the existence of any homework they don't understand because asking mom or dad even the simplest question is tantamount to opening Pandora's box. Their well-meaning parents can't contain their enthusiasm to turn what would ordinary require a short answer into a long-winded treatise on some esoteric detail.

Here's an example. How do you spell enlightenment? Instead of spelling the word, which will take all of three seconds, this parent may decide this is the perfect time to explore the wonderful world of prefixes, suffixes, and roots with their child who is trying to plow through an already overly long assignment. The parent's lesson is valuable, and is worth discussing at a more opportune time, but not during homework crunch time.

7. The child is unmotivated.

Most children don't want to do homework. But while they may put up quite a fuss, somehow they manage to get the work done. If they don't, motivation may not be the problem; instead it may be one or more of the other items on this list. They may appear unmotivated, but this may be a convincing protective screen they've set up to mask a larger issue.

Many children appear unmotivated when in fact they avoid homework to protect their egos. How's that? Because these children erroneously equate failure with stupidity. Their logic is as follows: If they try and fail, it is a reflection of their intelligence. If they don't try and fail, it is not a re-flection of their intelligence; it is due to lack of motivation or irresponsibility. *These* labels they can live with; the label "stupid," they can't!

8. Too much homework.

Many kids simply cannot keep up with the projects, tests, quizzes, reading and other assignments they are given.

Here is a general guide for the typical amount of time children should be expected to spend on homework each school day. Grades K-2, about 10-20 minutes. Grades 3-6, about 30-60 minutes. Grades 7-12 will vary considerably, depending on subjects, projects due, tests, etc., but a reasonable average is about two hours, with more on weekends, as needed, for major projects and exams.

If your child spends considerably more than this on homework, look into the cause. Begin by having a conversation with the teacher. If the problem is class-wide, hopefully the teacher will make adjustments. If the problem is limited to your child because your child works slowly, or has other issues discussed in this section, talk to his teacher and see what can be done to modify his assignments.

9. It's too noisy.

Many kids complain that they can't concentrate at home. Their siblings are running around, TVs and music systems are blaring, someone's on the phone, people are fighting, the dog is barking, the baby is crying. I don't know about you, but I need quiet to do work that requires thinking and, in fact, so do most people. Closed bedroom doors don't help much, as the muffled sounds of chaos always manage to get through.

Here is an idealistic solution. Even if it can't be carried out fully, at least it is something to aim for. As a family, consider designating a block of time to be quiet time. Normal living continues, but more quietly than usual. Kids can use the time to do homework—parents can read, balance the checkbook, and write e-mails; those who have time to watch television can do so with headphones or the sound turned low. Sometimes quiet sounds pretty good, doesn't it?

10. The child is too alone.

Some children are lonely when required to do homework in their rooms, and don't work efficiently in that setting. Some need continuous support and direction. That is, they need someone to help them stay on task or to provide a little assistance when they get stuck. If required to work alone in their rooms, these are the kids who emerge three hours later with little or nothing accomplished. Both groups of children tend to prefer doing homework on the kitchen table. This way they have people around them, either for support or company.

Okay. Now that you've solved all the homework-related issues in your household...

Of course, we're not serious. In the real world, in spite of everyone's best intentions, homework crises will still pop up. This is where the issue of trust comes in, but this time from another direction; your child has to trust that *you* will be there for *him.*

It only makes sense. Don't we turn to our kids when we need help cleaning up the house before company arrives? Or taking out the garbage? Or walking the dog? Trust goes both ways; kids need to trust that you will be there for them when they need some help and in turn, they have to be trustworthy when you need them. We get so hung up on homework—and rules about doing it—that we sometimes forget that students are people first.

Let's say your child has an assignment that must be completed before bedtime, and it's getting pretty late. Perhaps it is an unreasonably long reading assignment, or there was a family crisis that took up much of the afternoon and evening. Teamwork may be the solution. Why not take turns reading? She reads a paragraph, then you read one or two, then she reads one, etc., until it is completed.

Help For the Overworked Parent

As a parent, you probably work hard, and long, and arrive home pretty tired. The same is basically true for your children. In spite of good intentions, there will be times your trusting relationships need a little boost. For example, at the end of one of these days you may find yourself expending a lot of energy being a "watchdog," and very short on patience. On such occasions, instead of letting your stress and temper get the best of you so you hear yourself barking, "Do your homework!" or "Shut off that blankety-blank TV," try to remember that you will get better results if you can get yourself to use positive, trusting language. You actually can do this and bring up the topic of schoolwork at the same time! For example, consider saying, "If you need any help with your homework, just tell me. But give me a little time to relax first so that I can unwind after work." You'll be surprised how kids work with you if they know you're not going to hassle them about school the minute they see you. Schoolwork is probably the last thing in the world your child wants to think or talk about when he gets home from school. So, if you mention it in a way that makes him feel comfortable about coming to you, then he will, when he's ready to. Your child will like being trusted and will be more inclined to work with you toward developing such trust in the future.

> **Your child will like being trusted and will tend to work toward deserving such trust in the future.**

Consider this scenario: Your child comes to you. He has a problem, request, or just something he wants to share with you. But you're busy. You are working, talking on the phone, or frantically trying to get dinner ready. Do you:

A. Shoo him away with a wave of your hand?
B. Scowl menacingly at him, hoping he takes the hint?
C. Screech, "Can't you see I'm busy!"?
D. Grab him by the arm, drag him to his room, and throw him in?

If you selected any of the choices, you need to take a step back and try one of the following approaches instead.

- Tell your child that he is very important to you, and that even though right now you are unable to, you will respond to him when you finish what you're doing.
- Tell your impatient child to hold his thought for now, or to write it down so he doesn't forget it. The two of you will get together as soon as possible.

Here are two interactions that illustrate the type of parent-child dialogue worth aiming for.

Parent 1: "I know you had a lot to tell me, and it took a long time for me to listen to you. I appreciate your patience."
Child 1: "That's okay."

Parent 2: "I'm sorry, Nicole, that I took a long time to get to your question. I understand your frustration and I apologize. I've had so much on my mind. Let's go sit down in the kitchen, have some hot cocoa, and talk about it."
Child 2: "Okay, today at school, my history teacher said…"

If your child does not agree to sit together at a later time, use words that serve to keep the dialogue open so that she doesn't take this incident as a message not to come to you with problems in the future. For example:

Child: "Forget it, I don't feel like talking about it anymore."
Parent: "Okay, well, let me know if you feel like talking about it later. I'll be happy to listen to what's on your mind."

or

"Are you sure? It really seemed like something was bothering you before. Be sure to remember what happened and I'll try to be there for you next time."

Remember: Trusting and trustworthy parents promote trusting and trustworthy children. So, follow through on your promises, stick to your agreements, and keep to yourself the little secrets your child has shared with you. If your child can anticipate and understand your actions, is treated in a consistent and predictable fashion, and sees that your promises and agreements are fulfilled, then he will learn to trust others and, in turn, become a trustworthy person.

Chapter 4

Teaching Responsibility

"Every morning I have to wash my face, get dressed, comb my hair, brush my teeth, and eat breakfast. And my mom wants me to feed the cat too! How many chores can a kid do? I probably have more chores than any ten-year-old in the world!"

Timothy — Age 10

Timothy — the most overworked ten-year-old in the world — was feeling pretty down. When I asked him about it, he lamented that he had had an argument with his mom before school, and that she was being unfair.

While Timothy's list of chores may have been reasonable for most ten-year-olds, Timothy was clearly overloaded. Since he had many learning and physical disabilities, taking care of himself in the morning — doing the "chores" on his list — was all he could handle. The thought of one extra responsibility, feeding the cat, catapulted him into overload. Without anyone realizing it, this one extra chore upset a delicate balance, which had already begun to take its toll on his schoolwork.

I called Timothy's mom to find out if he had begun any new activities that might have created new demands or responsibilities for him. She thought for a moment. "He started taking karate lessons a few months ago," she said, "and just last month he started taking drums at school."

For the average child, these changes may not have been significant. But Timothy could not handle all the new responsibilities: schoolwork, karate, drums, everyday chores, and now...the cat! We were able to restore the balance by temporarily reducing his responsibilities. His sister would feed the cat, and he agreed to postpone drum lessons until the summer. Since his responsibilities once again matched his ability, he was soon back to himself.

While Timothy was having trouble managing his responsibilities at home, another student, Elliot, was having difficulty owning up to his responsibilities at school.

Elliot — Age 14

Elliot's parents brought him to my office for me to help him with his study skills. As I suspected that Elliot had Attention-Deficit/ Hyperactivity Disorder (ADHD), I referred him to a psychiatrist. The psychiatrist wanted to place him on medication, but he and his parents were against this.

Everyone involved was happy to know the source of Elliot's school problems, and we all looked forward to Elliot improving in school, but that didn't happen. Instead, he went from doing poorly to doing terribly. Why? Elliot had stopped trying.

Unlike Timothy, Elliot wasn't overloaded with too much responsibility at home. He was simply avoiding his responsibilities at school, using his ADHD as a shield. He stopped trying in school because, well, he had ADHD. He had his mom's tacit support as she felt that maybe everyone expected too much from him. After all, he had ADHD.

I contacted his teachers to see what was happening in his classes. Every teacher reported the same thing: Elliot wasn't doing anything. He sat slouched in his seat, legs sprawled out into the aisle, facing the windows. When teachers asked him to open his book and follow along, Elliot would respond, "I can't; I can't concentrate; I have ADHD."

When I confronted Elliot as to why he wasn't doing his work, he told me the same thing, "I can't do any work. I've got ADHD!" I reminded him that he was failing, and asked him, "Don't you want to pass?" Elliot told me that if he didn't pass it was his teachers' fault because that meant they weren't doing their jobs.

Elliot is a perfect example of the child who does not accept responsibility and blames those around him for his failure. Choosing to overcome his ADHD without the use of medication, Elliot had also needed to accept the responsibility. It took some time for Elliot and his mom to begin to accept and deal with the responsibility instead of using his condition as an excuse. Together, his teachers and I helped him learn strategies that enabled Elliot to achieve on his own.

In addition, the school needed to provide a tight structure for Elliot. A guidance counselor began to monitor his work at school, and Mom and Dad began to monitor his work at home. But, even more importantly, Elliot realized that he had to do the work. There were times when he would need some extra support to get his work done, but he still had to do his part.

It is not uncommon for children who are being tutored to believe that since they are being tutored, they do not have to take any responsibility. They think that private instruction one hour a week is all they need and that's where their responsibility ends. They seem to be genuinely surprised when they continue to do poorly in school. It is only when they assume their responsibilities do they begin to succeed at school, which in turn will promote their feelings of self-worth.

Tutoring is analogous to dieting. Some people think that if they go to a diet center once a week, they'll lose weight. But if they are not responsible, and stop off on their way home to have a big piece of chocolate cake, they can't blame the diet center when they don't lose weight. They have to see that all the diet center can do is motivate them and teach them what they should or should not do; it is up to them to take responsibility for their weight loss. Similarly, when I tutor or counsel children, I can show them strategies that will help them to learn, or to read with comprehension, or to understand a subject; but they need to go home and do what it takes for them to understand and retain the material. They have to become responsible; they have to take ownership of their schoolwork. If they don't, parents need to investigate why. Like Timothy, they may be feeling overwhelmed; like Elliot, they may be using a condition as an excuse not to work or there may be some other reason.

Responsibility is a Prerequisite for School Success

Responsibility is a prerequisite to growth and development. We've seen that it is essential to the development of self-esteem, but it is also essential to the development of strong character.

Youngsters with high self-esteem and a sense of responsibility to self and to others are more likely to succeed in school than those whose high self-esteem carries no sense of responsibility. Furthermore, as adults, these youngsters are more likely to become assets to their community. In most cases, children who are encouraged to take on age-appropriate chores and responsibilities tend to grow more self-confident and self-reliant.

Keep in mind that people may have high self-esteem in spite of not being responsible to themselves, their families or communities. For example, a drug dealer may take pride in himself for being one of the best dealers in his community. He has, therefore, achieved in a domain in which he aspires to excel, in addition to being positively viewed by his unsavory significant others. But in spite of his high feeling of self-worth, such a person is clearly morally and socially irresponsible.

A more familiar example is the schoolyard bully. This child might brag of his prowess to his friends and, in their eyes, may even be something of a hero. The bully's peers are important significant others at this point in his life and, given their approbation, he may feel good about himself. He is not, however, demonstrating a sense of personal responsibility, nor is he developing one.

DJ — Age 14

Or consider the case of DJ, the cool, handsome ninth-grade class jock who was failing almost all his subjects. He was a cute kid with personality galore and high verbal intelligence, and was captain of the freshman football team. Because of his grades, his parents had gone through the usual rituals — punishing, bribing, lecturing, taking away his favorite activities. Nothing was working, and they were on the verge of giving up. Because his teachers liked him so much, they went out of their way to offer him extra help. But he never took them up on their offers.

DJ and I met a few times to help him learn appropriate work habits and study skills. He was making progress, but somehow DJ always had a reason for not accepting responsibility. Then one day DJ said something that finally revealed precisely where he was coming from. I was showing him how to preview material, explaining that by doing this he would be the first one in his class to raise his hand because he would have already gone over the material. He spontaneously blurted out, "No, I can't do that."

"Why?" I asked, a little bewildered.

"You see, I'm one of the coolest kids in ninth grade. All the girls really like me," he said seriously. "If I keep answering questions, they'll think I'm a geek. So, no way, I'm not raising my hand!"

We talked about ways to get his homework in and to get better grades on tests while still maintaining his cool image.

I met with his mom and dad after that session and explained to them that DJ had very high self-esteem because he had the admiration of his peer group. At this point in his life it was unlikely that he would give up this precious role. To him, his foremost responsibility was to keep up this image.

I worked closely with the family and DJ to help him to become a more responsible student. And, in spite of getting higher grades, DJ saw that he was still accepted by his peers, with his hero image still intact.

DJ is one example of a child whose feeling of self-esteem prevented him from becoming a more responsible student. As he learned to accept school responsibility he began to enjoy the rewards. By being responsible he gained even more self-confidence. By the way, he's a senior now and applying to college as a business major.

Ten Ways You Can Promote a Sense of Responsibility

1. Be a good role model.

Of course, this goes for everything. Your children watch everything you do. If they see you as responsible, they will be more inclined to be responsible.

2. Provide structure.

You can help your child focus and succeed by creating a structure in which he can succeed. He may agree to do his homework on Sunday, but it will increase the chances of him actually doing the work if he is obliged to add more structure by selecting a specific time on Sunday.

It may still not get done. In that case, give him the chance to respond instead of automatically putting him on the defensive. This is far more likely to produce the desired outcome than if you act disgusted and ground him. That would only tell him that he is incapable of being responsible enough to do the work. Instead, you can continue to work out the problem together, and you avoid any hostility. Threats and abuse may indeed get the schoolwork done for the moment, but will not help the long-term development of a responsible child.

3. Help your children with scheduling.

By creating lists, tally sheets or charts, your child can monitor her own progress on homework, chores or projects. This will remind her of the jobs she has yet to complete. It will also give her feelings of worth and pride when she sees a task has been completed. This in turn promotes a sense of responsibility and high self-esteem.

The following is a sample of an after school checklist for a middle- or high-schooler.

√	3:30-4:30	*Snack, watch television* (relax and unwind)
	4:30-6:00	*Do homework* (follow assignment book closely)
	6:00-7:00	*Dinner and chores* (decided upon together)
	7:00-8:00	*Finish homework* (if needed); *practice drums/karate*
	8:00-9:00	*Call & e-mail friends* (everyone needs some fun)

4. Avoid performing tasks children can do for themselves.

You may be surprised at what your child is capable of doing for herself if you allow her to tackle tasks you usually do for her. Parents sometimes continue to tie shoes, button coats or even clean out school backpacks for their children long after the kids are capable of doing such tasks themselves. Generally, the more they do on their own, the higher self-esteem they will have. Paradoxically, in many situations, the less you help your child, the more you help your child.

Once again, it's a fine line parents walk, so take care to gauge how much your child can handle. To help ourselves, even though it is difficult, we should put ourselves into our children's shoes, attempt to see things from their points of view. As in the case of Timothy, sometimes what seems normal to you may seem overwhelming to your child.

5. Allow your child to help you.

Invite him to work along with you to clean the kitchen, straighten up a room, take care of a pet, set the table, dust the furniture, or mow the lawn. He will enjoy helping you and being responsible — especially if you enjoy his company and remember not to criticize him if he slows you down or does a less-than-perfect job. This works particularly well if you are a bit creative with the tasks. (Remember Mary Poppins?) What child can resist a contest to see who can get the most clean laundry into the appropriate open drawers from across the room?

6. Avoid setting standards that your child may not be capable of achieving.

Do you demand B's or even A's in every subject? Are you telling your thirteen-year-old how important it is to get into an Ivy-league college? Then you are running the risk of dooming her to feeling like a failure even if she succeeds, for your expectations may be too specific and too high; or, if she meets those standards, she may be doing so for your benefit, not her own, so her success might not contribute to her self-esteem.

How do you know what your child is capable of? It is very difficult to judge. One way is to observe her as she performs the task in question. Evaluate if she is doing it correctly. If she consistently fails to perform certain tasks, you should not criticize her; instead, investigate the causes of this failure. Consider seeking ability and/or educational testing for school-related issues. Your child may not be emotionally, socially and/or intellectually developed enough to perform certain tasks, and you may need to change your expectations and/or help the child learn strategies that will help her to achieve.

7. Allow adequate time for training.

Like adults, children need time — to learn new things, to do chores, to finish their homework. It takes time to process new information. The youngster who is rushed may follow directions by mimicking what you are doing, but probably won't understand the significance of the task or process the new information.

Also, if you feel rushed, you may be applying pressure to your child, and she may become discouraged. So remember that building responsibility takes time. Your child will not immediately start feeding the dog, cleaning her room and setting the table every day without being reminded to do so. She will need plenty of encouragement and reminders. So take your time, allow for plenty of slip-ups, and remind yourself that your child needs lots of support, not punishment, in order to become responsible.

8. Be prepared to keep encouraging your child.

When a child is occasionally discouraged either by the weight of her responsibility or by her failure to be responsible, you can counteract such discouragement by reminding her of her successes in previously performed tasks. For example, if your child calls you at work, frantic from all the homework she has to do, and says, "I have so much homework, I don't think I can do it all," you may respond, "You know you always come through somehow. Why don't you make a list of everything you need to do. Remember we did that last time you had a lot of homework. Do only one thing at a time, like you did last time. If you get stuck on anything leave it, and Daddy or I will help you when we get home. And, don't become overwhelmed. You always manage. I'm always impressed with how well you handle all this work."

9. Emphasize the logical consequences of irresponsible behavior.

Once you are certain that your child is capable of performing a task and has had enough time to do so, he needs to experience the consequences (the effects) of irresponsibility (the cause). These consequences should be neither punitive nor abusive.

Let's return, for a moment, to the example about Sunday night homework. Let's assume that in spite of your efforts your child doesn't do his homework. There comes a point that you have to make difficult decisions. While it may be tempting for you to do the homework for him out of frustration, this is an unacceptable choice because in effect, all you'll be doing is showing him that he is untrustworthy, and he will learn that he can be irresponsible without any real consequences.

That leaves the choice of letting him experience the consequences of his irresponsibility. For now, simply extricate yourself from the situation and let whatever happens happen—no yelling, no dirty looks—just let it be. The consequences for an occasional responsibility-mishap may be minor; he may get away with it, but it is more likely that he will receive a zero for the assignment and possibly fail the next test. His irresponsible behavior may even spin out of control and he may have to experience the heavy hand of logical consequences: he may fail the course and have to make it up in summer or night school, double up next year or be retained. Some children need to see first hand that they are not invincible, that there are real consequences for irresponsible behavior.

Also while on the subject of homework, it's worth mentioning that as we explored in Chapter 3, there are many reasons why children avoid homework. While irresponsibility is certainly a possible cause, it may only appear that way; the cause may lie elsewhere.

10. Help your children become responsible by establishing rules that are fair, sensible and easy to follow.

"We've taken his driving license away for so long that, unless he shapes up, we'll be driving him around until he's forty."

Parents of Brett—Age 16

According to his mother, Brett was "failing everything." It didn't take long for me to learn that their rule for Brett was that he was to "bring home" B's or better. Nothing lower than a B was acceptable.

Both Mom and Dad were clearly disgusted with Brett, repeatedly referring to him as lazy. I asked them if there was room for C's, or maybe even an occasional D. "Of course not," they both agreed. "He's quite capable of being an A+ student, but we'll take B's if we have to." It seemed important to Mom and Dad that I know that Brett had been in the Gifted and Talented program in elementary school and that Dad was a graduate of a prestigious law school. They mentioned these facts several times.

Brett was clearly angry with his parents for taking away his license for so long. He wasn't sure he would ever be allowed to drive again! Whenever he got below an 85 on a test, his parents went ballistic. Besides taking away his television, telephone, and computer, they added more time to his wheel-less condition. One line of Brett's was particularly revealing: "So, why bother," he said. "I can't please them anyway." Brett was one burnt-out, angry, defiant eleventh-grader.

Our schools are full of Bretts: high-potential kids who are failing or getting poor grades. Brett's parents were obsessed with their rules, totally disregarding their child's needs and abilities. Their goals were unrealistic, and their unyielding boundaries were based on those unrealistic goals.

Brett was bright, but he had many issues that prevented him from reaching his potential. He was very disorganized, unable to manage his time well, over-extended socially, and over-extended in sports. If he was to succeed in school, he needed to learn organizational and time-management skills. He also needed to evaluate which sports and social events meant the most to him, so he could eliminate the less important activities. Brett had to learn how to prioritize, a cognitive skill that was difficult for him. (Recent brain research shows that the portion of the brain responsible for this function is not yet fully developed in teenagers.) With my intervention, Brett and his parents began to understand the cause of his difficulties. Things began to improve when Brett made some big decisions that opened up his schedule. We worked on his organizational and time-management skills too. But the biggest breakthrough was that I was able to get his parents to see that they had to change also. They came to realize the extent to which their illogical boundaries had caused Brett to shut down, and they changed accordingly. Soon his grades improved to A's and B's. And now, on those few occasions when Brett does poorly, he and his parents focus on the cause of the problem, and deal with it in a logical way. Oh yes, and he now gets to use the car.

Rules About Rules

We all need rules, children and adults alike. They serve as boundaries to establish what is and is not acceptable behavior. Parents begin setting boundaries for their children from the time their children are born. To be effective, the rules need to be well thought out, logical, and fair to all involved.

> **To be effective, rules need to be well thought out, logical, and fair to all involved.**

- **Be sure your rules make sense.**

When moms and dads create rules, they have the best intentions. However, sometimes the rules, especially those that were created on the fly, are arbitrary and illogical. Such rules need to be evaluated and modified. This should not be interpreted as caving-in on the part of parents, but as part of a natural, evolving family process.

Sara — Age 13

Sara's dad had set a rule that she had to sit at the dining room table for four hours every Saturday and Sunday to study. After I gasped for breath, I asked him a series of questions that included: "How did you decide that an eighth grader needs four hours? Did anyone teach her how to study? How do you know she's learning anything? What are the other family members doing during those four hours?"

It seems that while his daughter sits at the dining room table for the four hours doing something that, to a nontrained observer, resembles schoolwork, her mom is in the kitchen talking on the phone, her two younger brothers are playing noisily in the playroom near the kitchen, and dad is in the next room watching television and yelling at her brothers to keep quiet. His rationale is that it took him until his twenties to mature and succeed in school, and he wasn't letting this happen to his children. He started this weekend routine when she was in fifth grade and, no matter how much she cried, he wouldn't budge. He indicated that he intended to do the same with his boys when they reach fifth grade. I asked him, "Is it working?" Reluctantly, he admitted that it was not.

Like many well-meaning parents, Sara's dad had a wonderful goal for his children. But the approach he had selected to solve one problem was creating a much more severe problem in another area. Unwittingly, his role had gradually changed from parent to parole officer.

- **Be sure your children understand the logic behind your rules.**

It is easy for parents, and adults in general, to assume that children understand the logic behind rules. But often they do not. As they are more inclined to obey rules if they understand the logic behind them, it is a good idea to explain to them the rationale behind your rules, and not just say, "Because I said so."

For young children, you might have to begin with the basics, the cause-and-effect logic behind some common rules. What would happen if cars could drive on the left and right sides of roads? What would happen if cars didn't stop for red lights? What would happen if everyone spoke at the same time? What would happen if kids could eat just candy for breakfast, lunch and supper? Once they see the ramifications of a world without rules, it will be easier for them to understand the logic behind the specific rules they encounter on a daily basis.

For example, many parents limit the time their children can spend playing computer games. As they are obsessed with the games, they *hate* this rule. A chat about the logic of that rule has proven valuable over and over when kids have come to me disgruntled because they weren't allowed to play their games. An amazing transformation often happens when I share with them how current brain research applies to them. I point out that the teenage brain is still developing—as in, still growing new brain cells! So if all they do all day is play shoot-em-up computer games, their brains will grow so that they're only good at computer games. Amazing as it sounds, one youngster transformed himself instantly, and actually began to read on his own time. Later, when I asked him why, he told me he'd gotten scared — that his father had never learned how to read, and he didn't want that to happen to him. Once kids understand the cause-and-effect relationship between a rule and their lives, they see that they have power and control over their own destinies.

- **Be sure that your rules are fair.**

Children should be part of the rule-evaluation process. After sharing input with your child about one of your rules, you may have to do some serious soul-searching, evaluating some of the questions that arise. Ask yourself if a rule has been established for your child's benefit or for your convenience.

Nathaniel — Age 9

Nathaniel is the oldest of three children. His mom complained that he took forever to do his homework. Her rule was that all homework needed to be completed immediately after school. She said that the evenings were too hectic, with the laundry, the dishes, bath time and preparing for the next day.

From her point of view, it was a very sensible rule. Yet, after talking to Nathaniel, I learned that he had trouble concentrating after school because he knew his friends were out playing and he wanted to be with them. He also needed to let some energy out after a long day spent in classrooms. His mother was rather rigid; she insisted that her way was best. I reminded her that if it were working, she wouldn't be in my office. She laughed at that.

The three of us worked out a schedule for each day of the week and decided which time each day would be the best time for Nathaniel to do his homework. Mom also changed her laundry schedule and hired the teenager next door to help him with his homework.

Many parents question how they will know if rules are too strict or too lax. The answer is simple: your children will let you know by their behavior. For example, they may act out, become defiant, cry or become sad. When that happens, talk to them about it, and see if you can arrive at a solution that will be both effective and fair.

- **When your child breaks a rule, find out why!**

Sometimes parents and teachers punish children for breaking rules without first looking into the reasons why they broke them. They may say, "Why'd you do that?" He may be so intimidated that he can't think of saying anything more than, "I don't know." Then the parent will punish and say, "Well, next time you'll know." Needless to say, this is an ineffective way to respond to the breaking of a rule.

Dennis — Age 8

Early in our first session Dennis blurted out that he had to go straight home after he finished with our work because he had stolen some Tootsie Rolls® from the teacher's desk and was being grounded. As this was our first session, both parents were present. Dad commented about not being able to trust him and Mom added something about being disappointed. Later, I asked Dennis why he took the candy. His explanation was pretty sad. It seems that for some reason, no one played with him at recess. He thought if he gave candy to the kids, they would play with him. Dennis's eight-year-old brain did

77

not allow him to understand the significance of his own behavior. Punishing him did not help him understand, nor did it help him deal with the underlying problem.

What could Dennis's parents have done differently? At an opportune time and place, they could have talked to him in a non-threatening way to learn why he took the candy. Dennis would have most likely opened up, and they could have begun to unravel and resolve the issues together.

The issue of friendship. Once his parents saw the problem he was having with getting friends, they could have helped him set up play dates with the kids in his class. Perhaps Dennis could have invited one or two of his classmates to go bowling or to the movies. The important thing is that by talking with Dennis, they could have gotten to the underlying issue—that Dennis needed friends. They also may have explored what he may have been doing to turn off other kids, whether it be annoying mannerisms, poor personal hygiene, or his insecure behavior. It may be that he simply needed to learn a few ground rules on how to be a good friend. Mom and Dad could have borrowed or bought a children's book about friendship that they could have read and discussed with their son.

The issue of stealing. They also needed to talk to Dennis about the realities of stealing (even just a candy bar) and the real-world consequences of such an act. This time, since the issue was not primarily about stealing but the need for friends and belonging, his parents might do well to take Dennis to the store to buy replacement candies, and have him bring them to the teacher with a note of apology that Dennis writes himself. Writing the note himself is likely enough punishment in this case. If this negative behavior were to continue, his parents would do well to seek professional help.

One of the most difficult parts of this rule-establishing business is avoiding the temptation to pull rank: "I'm the parent, so I can do whatever I want." While this may be true in some areas, in others it creates a double standard, which sets the stage for big family problems. The phrase, "Do as I say, not as I do" is steeped in conflict from the very beginning. The child just doesn't see it that way. The child sees "unfair" written all over the rules, and resents the double standard.

Since family harmony is a prized commodity, parents need to keep in mind the adage "actions speak louder than words." If you watch daytime soaps on Friday and three football games in a row on Sunday while stretched out on the couch, how can you then impose a "no TV" rule for your child? Many children complain that they can't watch TV during the week—that's the rule. But then they tell me that they can't concentrate on their homework because Dad is watching TV and he makes it loud. It's easy to see the problem here. But when I suggest to the parents that they curtail their viewing for the sake of their children, they look at me as if I have two heads. "We're tired and need time to relax too," they say. Well, that's true. But they are teaching their children to have double standards and to disrespect the feelings and needs of others. Therefore, I ask them to reevaluate their rules and goals as parents. If their goal is to have an educated, responsible, well-adjusted child, they all may need to work together, sometimes making sacrifices, to achieve that goal. Will it be easy? No. As my grandmother used to say, "Bringing up children is not as easy as eating an apple."

Chapter 5

Providing Options

"Stop telling me what to do!"
Angela — Age 16

Mrs. Wingfield brought her daughter Angela to our office in the middle of the school year. Mrs. Wingfield was a single parent whose husband had died in an accident when Angela was four. The school psychologist had referred Angela to us because she had morphed from a perfect little elementary school student to a rebellious, angry and defiant tenth-grader. Angela had failed two of her ninth-grade courses (which she had made up in summer school), and was currently failing three out of her five tenth-grade courses. In addition to her school problems, it appeared that she had befriended every teenager who had gone astray, assuming the role of rescuer-advisor-counselor to her new friends.

"Maaa-ah, you don't understand," Angela whined when her mom described the situation at home to me. "Julie hates her stepfather! She has to talk to me whenever — "

"No, young lady, you don't understand," her mother barked back, cutting her off in mid-sentence. "Julie is not my problem. You are. I have to watch over you and that's enough."

"Just leave me alone," snapped Angela as she turned sideways on the chair.

When we made eye contact I said, "You must hate school. Isn't it hard? So many kids that come here complain that it's so hard — and boring."

Angela turned to face me. "Yeah, it's horrible. And the teachers are so mean. Like if you talk to your friend just one time, they kick you out of class."

"Oh, really," said Mrs. Wingfield, raising an eyebrow. "You didn't tell me about that. When did that happen?"

"I don't have to tell you everything," snapped Angela. "Anyway I had to talk to Steve then. He had just broken up with Shaunna and he needed my advice."

"Oh, I'm sure you gave him great advice," her mother answered sarcastically. "You can't even choose the right clothes to wear and you're deciding things for others. That's a good one."

I pulled the conversation back to her schoolwork by asking Angela what she did when she first realized she was failing in ninth grade.

"What?" she said, surprised.

"When you started to fail in math last year, what did you do?" I asked.

"What do you mean? I didn't do anything," she replied.

"What could you have done to start passing?" I asked.

"I don't know," she answered.

"Could you have gone to the teacher?" I asked calmly.

"Yeah, I guess. But I wouldn't. I hate him," she said in a hostile tone.

"Could you have gone to your counselor?" I asked.

"I guess I could have," she said.

"Could you have gone to your Mom?" I asked.

"NO!" she said quickly. "She'd just ground me again."

"So let me get this straight," I said. "You were failing math. Do you want to fail math?"

"Of course not," she said emphatically.

"So, let's see what options you had so that you could pass. Sometimes it's easier to write them," I said, as I handed her this chart.

Problem	Option 1	Option 2	Option 3

I told Mom that if she didn't mind, I'd like Angela to fill in the chart without her help. Mom was taken aback. She sat back hesitantly and let me fill in the chart with Angela.

We began by selecting one problem: her failing grades in math. We wrote down several options that Angela could have tried in order to pass.

For the second problem, I suggested we turn our attention to the English class she had failed. She told us that she liked her English teacher, but never thought of going to talk to her. Together we filled in several options. Angela was able to evaluate the options for each problem and select the ones she would try.

Problem	Option 1	Option 2	Option 3
1. Failing math	Get help from Mom	Get help from Mr. Sinozzi [her teacher] or Mary Jo [her tutor]	Get help from Shaunna [her friend who is good at Math]
2. Failing English	Get help from Mom	Get help from Ms. Hannigan or Mary Jo	Get help from Eric [her friend who excels in English]

I asked Angela if she could think of any other problem we needed to talk about. She said no. Angela had no idea that the inordinate amount of time she spent counseling her friends was a way for her to avoid dealing with her own school problems. She had not yet perceived that this was a problem in itself.

Angela's mom was right. Angela *had been* the perfect little girl, all through elementary school and middle school. Then, she had earned straight A's (which, Mom boasted, she got without picking up a book), she was the teacher's pet, and, in general, did whatever Mom wanted. If Mom told her little girl to wear the pink-and-green outfit, then it was the pink-and-green outfit that Angela wore. If Mom said they were having lima beans for dinner, even though Angela hated lima beans, then they had lima beans for dinner. It seems that Angela had few opportunities to learn how to make decisions; she just went along with her domineering Mom.

Since this was a family problem, both Angela and her mom had to learn that there were a few issues to deal with. Both had to change a little.

To begin with, they had to understand that there was nothing wrong with Angela; she was a normal teenager. At her age, her brain was neither fully developed nor fully integrated. In general, the parts of the teenage brain that are responsible for emotions are developed and highly active, while the portions of the brain responsible for planning and cognition are far less developed. At a recent conference on brain research, one lecturer jokingly referred to young teenagers as "sacks of emotions on two legs."

Second, Mom had to learn to let go. She was no longer the only important significant other in her teenager's life. Her daughter's peers and teachers had an increasingly influential role now.

Third, Mom had to establish a better relationship with Angela so that she would feel comfortable — and safe — coming to her for help.

Finally, Angela had to learn decision-making skills. Now that she was in high school, she had to learn how to identify and evaluate *options* so that she could make her own informed decisions. Had Mom not dominated the decision-making from the time she was little, Angela probably would have become adept at making decisions, and wouldn't have felt so trapped; instead, she would have been able to use those skills to develop the strategies she needed in order to succeed in high school and beyond.

How to Help Your Child to Develop Decision-Making Skills

* **Provide opportunities for your child to make decisions.**

When a situation arises that involves options, and it is an appropriate issue for your child to be involved in, include her in the decision-making process. Discuss or write down the pros and cons of the various options. With a young child, you might discuss a decision about whether to go to the amusement park or beach over the weekend. With an older child, you might discuss the pros and cons of private school versus public school.

These decisions need to be based on your child's age and capabilities. For example, four-year-old Tracie can decide whether she prefers spinach or string beans for a vegetable, but not whether she would like a vegetable or ice cream. Sam, a little first-grader, can decide which of three types of cookies he wanted for a snack. And a fifth-grader, Amanda, can decide whether or not she should play on the softball team.

* **Encourage everyone to participate in decisions regarding family activities.**

Too often parents decide the activities, and children are forced to go along. It's much more fun when everyone is in on the decision! For example, the whole family could decide which restaurant to dine at or which movie to see on the weekend.

When children contribute to decisions on family activities, it promotes their feelings of self-worth and invests them in the activity; then they will be more inclined to enjoy themselves. Even if after participating in the decision-making process they end up hating the activity, that will teach them about the consequences and responsibilities of decision-making; things don't always go the way we hope they will!

- **Discuss real-life decision-making situations.**

Talk about the news, read stories, and watch videos dealing with real-life issues; afterwards, discuss the decisions the key players made. Someday, your child will have to make important decisions at every turn. So if you discuss potential choices that arise, or point out the decisions kids make in movies, television shows and books, your child will be better prepared when he'll have to make major decisions by himself. If, for example, Angela and her Mom had worked together in the past, discussing options for different decisions that arose, Angela might have thought to discuss her high-school problems with her mom. But Angela had not even considered that an option.

Of course, sometimes children and teens have too much control, as in the case of Wally, a student in my class when I was a first year teacher. Wally, a slightly smaller than average third grader got up for show and tell. He pulled a little pillbox out of his pocket and said that if his mom took these pills, she would not have a baby. He went on to explain that his mom wanted another baby, but his dad and his older sister and he wanted a boat instead. With that, he put the pillbox back in his pocket and sat down. The twenty-five other third graders sat and stared at him without the usual comments and questions. I too just sat and stared. My mind raced for something to say, but all that I could think of was "Next!"

The point? Wally was growing up in a family where considering options was an integral part of his development. He saw himself as part of a family that discussed everything openly, and so didn't see anything unusual in sharing the family decisions with his class — even their decision to have a baby!

Learning how to make decisions in various situations gives children control over their lives, and encourages them to be responsible for their behavior — all of which is integral to the lifestyle of the successfully functioning student and adult.

The following are some areas in which you can help your children learn how to evaluate options and make good decisions:

- **For younger children**

Selecting clothing — Children can choose their own clothing provided it's appropriate for the weather and occasion. They may also help to choose some of the clothes you buy for them. Talk about seasons — warm clothes and cool clothes. If a child insists on wearing a pink shirt, green pants and orange hat, let it go if it's not going to cause a huge problem — for example, if you're all going to a wedding. In that case you can discuss appropriate attire for "special occasions" like weddings, religious services, and school plays. When he's older, you can start to talk about fashion and style. He may even get the message sooner, if the kids start making fun of him for his lack of color sense.

Selecting family activities — If children are knowledgeable, they can make better decisions. If they have the choice between a movie, a day at the park with Dad or visiting Grandma, they may choose to visit Grandma if they know it will make her happy and that the following week they can go to the movies. You might help your children make decisions by having them say or write the pros and cons for each activity.

- **For middle-school students**

Middle-schoolers can make decisions about after-school activities, sports, volunteer projects, hairstyles, even some classes such as which foreign language to take. Help them make informed choices by having them use the Internet, visit the library, poll your adult friends and relatives, talk to their friends. Examples:

Hair styles — Kids can look at fashion magazines, get opinions about what may flatter their faces, look at the pros and cons of various hair styles.

Selecting school electives — If they have a choice between French and Spanish, have them talk to people who took both languages; use the Internet to find out in what countries these languages are spoken and what job opportunities may arise if someone is fluent in a language; talk to the teachers of both languages to get an idea of how hard they might be for them to learn.

- **For high school students**

High-school students will be making lots of choices — about careers, dating, social situations, and peer pressure.

Role-play — Have your teen role-play responses to certain situations — maybe with a good friend or two or, more likely, just by herself. Role playing by yourself is not as weird as it sounds. After thinking about what "he" would say, switch modes and think of what "she" would — or should — say. Examples: she is driving with a friend who hands her a bottle of beer; a boyfriend is pressuring her to have sex; all of her friends smoke and it's getting hard to resist their offers to "try a drag just once."

Career choices — Teens can start looking at careers and thinking about the skills and talents they have. Help them with an interest inventory, and let them know they can make the most of their strengths.

Learning how to make decisions in various situations gives children control over their lives, and encourages them to be responsible for their behavior—all of which is integral to the lifestyle of the successfully functioning student and adult.

"Ma, I weighed my options, just like you said.
I decided to stop taking tests."

Chapter 6

Meeting Needs

"I don't know why I keep getting such bad grades. I study every night until 1:00 AM."
Anthony — Age 16

Anthony was feeling pretty poorly about himself. He felt that there was something wrong with him. No matter how much he studied, he still got C's.

After completing a week's schedule to see how much time he spent actually studying, we discovered that the problem wasn't the amount of time he studied; the problem was his physical condition. He didn't have the energy to study. He was on the lacrosse team, which had lengthy practice sessions every day after school. He then went to work at the supermarket, because he wanted money to pay for his car. He said he never ate breakfast because he woke up too late, so he would grab a candy bar or donut on his way to school.

Anthony, like Walter from Chapter 1—and untold numbers of teens like them—was neglecting three important health needs: he was not eating properly; he was physically exhausted; and he was not getting adequate sleep. Once he realized that he was causing his own problems, it was easy for him to remedy them himself.

**As a parent, it is your job to see that
your child's basic needs are met.**

The Need to Eat Well

There is no escaping the fact that your child needs a balanced diet with all food groups represented. You can gradually introduce a variety of new foods to your meals. And while it's never too late, the earlier you start in a child's life, the easier this is. If the food looks and tastes good, you'll find ready and willing participants. Remember too to set a good example with the foods you eat and the foods you make available to the family. For the meals you make at home, the bookstores and Internet are chock full of healthful recipes for kid-friendly dishes; and perhaps your child can even help prepare the meal. We understand that getting teenagers to eat well is often difficult. I have seen many teenagers who are overly concerned with their image or are simply too busy to eat properly. This is a problem, as your child's brain and body need energy and nutrients, so, as a result, they do not have the mental or physical strength to study and succeed in school.

Skipping breakfast is probably the most common issue for teenagers. School mornings are such a whirlwind that many kids rush out of the house without eating anything. There are many quick and easy solutions, but here is one that works particularly well—a glass of milk and a little bag of not-too-sweet cold cereal. It takes almost no time to down the milk. Eating the cold cereal from the bag en route completes the breakfast without taking much additional time.

The Need for Adequate Sleep

Fact: The average teen needs over nine hours of sleep each night and younger children need even more.

Sleep deprivation, while a possible issue for children of any age, is particularly prevalent in teenagers. It can make teens cranky and blue, ruin their concentration, delay their response time in critical situations such as driving, and eventually affect their health. But the average teen today rarely gets enough sleep. They tend to stay up late, then have to wake up early to catch their school bus. But it's not enough to say to them, "Get to sleep earlier." The truth is that teens really can't go to sleep that early. Their biological clocks won't let them. But you can be an ally. Help your children adjust their schedules so that they are not doing homework late at night, allow them to sleep in on the weekends so they can catch up a bit and campaign for later school starting times. Think about it. Asking our teens to wake up at 5:30 a.m. to get dressed and catch a school bus at 6:30 is ridiculous when they go to sleep after 11:00.

As for young children, you can be the judge of what's an appropriate bedtime for your child. You see how tired they get during the day and you know how difficult it is to wake them in the morning.

If falling asleep is an issue, here are some tips from the National Sleep Foundation you can share with your children.

- **Exercise regularly, but not too close to bedtime.** Late-day physical activity tends to keep your body awake.
- **Create a pleasant sleep environment —** comfortable, dark and as quiet as possible.

- **Establish a regular bedtime** so you can unwind and signal your brain that it's time to sleep.
- **Consider using the bed just for sleeping.** If children or teens do homework or watch TV in bed, their bodies may be telling them to be alert rather than go to sleep.
- **Do something relaxing before going to sleep.** Take a bath, read, be read to. If a child has something on her mind, tell her to write it down in a "worry book" to work on the next day. Problems often seem smaller in daylight.
- **Avoid caffeine late in the day.** Caffeine has found its way into the regimen of many children from such sources as cola, cold coffee drinks, and high-energy drinks. If lack of sleep is an issue, check to see if caffeine is the problem.

A lack of sleep is often at the root of school problems. If your child has ongoing problems sleeping and you can't figure out why, seek professional advice.

The Need for Adequate Physical Activity

Maybe you run to the gym after work, during lunch or at sunrise. But the fact is, your children need to be active, too. Along with proper nutrition, the health benefits from regular physical activity are startling: it promotes a sense of well-being; reduces the risk for serious health problems such as high blood pressure and diabetes; helps build and maintain healthier bones, muscles and joints; controls weight; and is a great stress-buster. Activity stimulates the whole body, including the brain, which in turn helps children focus, process and learn. Even a half hour of moderate activity on most days can be beneficial, though health experts recommend more.

Tips for promoting physical activity

- **Let your child choose his activities.** No sense asking him to do something he hates. You can offer suggestions and options, but it has to be his choice in the end.
- **Allow your child to run, jump, leap and climb.** Physical activity involves movement, so active play can be good. Glob sunscreen on your child and possibly insect repellent on his clothing and encourage him to play outside.
- **Do things as a family.** Go bowling, play basketball, take a walk. Show your child that you value physical activity too.
- **Encourage your child to participate in school sports**, but only if he's interested in being on a team and likes to compete. If he finds out the sport is not for him, it's okay to drop out and try something else.
- **Make it fun.** Let your teen have friends over on rainy nights to learn new dance steps; play Frisbee® in the yard; do couch-potato workouts during your favorite TV show: five-minute warm-ups before the show; stretches, weight lifts and ab curls during the segments; cardio (run up and down stairs, jump rope) during commercials; and then cool down before the next show. Variations of these are also great for kids who have difficulty staying seated for long periods of time. Also, they might benefit by doing them between homework assignments.

The Need to Manage Stress Effectively

An alarming number of children today are experiencing stress-related problems that hamper their school success. They don't have much time for play; they have more homework than in the recent past; and their homes, with overstressed working parents, are no longer the sanctuaries they once might have been. Their stress prevents them from concentrating, from relaxing, from studying properly, from sleeping; thus, it hinders them from succeeding in school.

Naturally, the amount and nature of stress determines how much it affects the child. Certain circumstances could create such stress that it overwhelms a child. As a fourteen-year-old once complained to me, "My mother died and my father is about to marry someone I hate. How am I supposed to do school?"

You are probably not a trained psychologist. Nonetheless, you are your child's primary personal counselor—not an easy role. But you can seek help from books like this one, and from others you can find in your local library and bookstore. Their shelves are stacked with children's books and young-adult books that deal exclusively with stress-related material. However, sometimes your child, as well as you, can become so stressed out that you feel as if you're in over your head. At such times, don't be embarrassed to seek professional help; professionals themselves seek help when they are stressed!

And remember to have fun. The lives of some children are not only stressful, but joyless. They feel pressure at school, and home life is gloomy because their parents are stressed out and unhappy. They are denied the kind of fun that should be a natural part of childhood. When you think back on your childhood, what comes to mind are probably feelings—of sadness, happiness, fear, love—and memories of fun and sad times you spent with your family. What will your child feel, or remember, when she thinks back on her childhood? Having fun is a necessary element of a child's development and essential to her happiness.

Suggestions for fun days:

- **Share funny stories** about real personal experiences from the past. They help kids learn to laugh at themselves.
- **Go on family outings** and vacations that everyone will enjoy.
- **Attend movies, plays, school functions or local shows together.**
- **Take in sports events,** whether at the local high school or a large stadium.
- **Play board games or computer games.** Get out the old Monopoly®, Sorry!® or Scrabble® box and cajole everyone in the house to play. Try Pictionary® or charades, or some other games that are somewhat physical — they're fun and there's some action too. As for computer games, children typically are vastly superior to their parents, and this makes them feel good about themselves. You wouldn't hesitate to engage your child in a game at which you are an expert; so give him the same chance! And, oh yes, how about giving family karaoke a try?
- **Prepare a special meal together.** Create ways to involve your child in the meal, or let him spice up an everyday dish with an unexpected addition. He won't believe how great his culinary masterpiece will taste!

- **Plan a holiday or birthday party together.** You may think you know what your child wants for his birthday celebration, but ask him instead—he may have an idea that you haven't thought of. As a consequence he will relish the memory of his special day.

- **Share a joke a day**—at breakfast, dinner, or via email.

- **Be sure that you have fun, too.** Remember, your child is aware of the foods you eat, the rest you get, the exercising you do or do not do, and the degree to which you try to enjoy life. As a role model you are never off duty. It behooves you, therefore, to set a good example and enjoy your own life. Make sure that parenting doesn't become an all-consuming task for you. You might feel guilty about leaving your child with a babysitter as you go out to dinner with your spouse, or see a play with a good friend, or play tennis, but by setting aside time for your own fun, you are showing your child that you know how to be happy, and how to take time out to enjoy your life.

The Need to Learn Effective Study Skills

School age children and teens think they know how to study. Our experience shows that most students don't use the most efficient study methods—the ones that best match their learning styles. Worse than that, some never learned how to study at all. The result: children end up spending countless hours studying each night—with all the slamming, yelling and crying that entails—only to do poorly. It is surprising how many good kids end up with bad grades simply because they don't know how to study.

Lori — Age 12

It was a hot summer day in early July when I first met Lori, a quiet little girl who was soon to begin eighth grade. She had failed science and social studies in seventh grade and was very anxious about starting a new school year. Her mom and dad said that they had worked with her for hours before each test and she still failed. It was soon clear that there was basically nothing wrong: Lori was above average in intelligence, she didn't have any learning disabilities, her basic needs were not an issue, and she seemed to work well with her parents. There shouldn't have been any problems, and yet she failed.

Lori had not learned how to study and her parents, in spite of their good intentions, didn't know how to teach her.

I worked with Lori one hour each week during the summer. Often one — and sometimes both — of her parents remained during the sessions. Basically, all Lori needed was to learn study skills. I showed her how to apply them using the science and social studies topics that had given her so much trouble. Since these new study skills closely matched her learning style, she picked them up with ease.

Of all the study skills I taught her, previewing was the one that seemed to help her the most. Previewing involves quickly looking ahead at the material that will be taught in school the next day. I shared with her the analogy I always use in my talks. Imagine going to an opera without first learning what it is about, perhaps from one of the short summaries that are readily available. If you are like most people, you wouldn't have any idea what it is about, and as a result you'd probably spend much of the time staring at the chandeliers, not getting much out of the experience.

What I showed Lori is to look over the vocabulary and concepts before the teacher's presentation in class. I then showed her another skill that she liked, chunking. This is grouping large amounts of material into chunks of four or five pieces so they are easier to learn. I explained that the brain can only process small chunks at a time. In fact, that is the reason postal zip codes only have five digits. Lori also enjoyed using multisensory strategies. That means using as many senses as appropriate when learning new material — including seeing, writing, drawing quick pictures, using graphic organizers and rephrasing (explaining it in her own words). When the school year began Lori was now anxious — in a positive sense. She told me she couldn't believe she was saying it, but she couldn't wait for school to start. She got a 98% on her first test and continued to do well in school!

Studying according to your needs works wonders!

Study Skills Tips

- **When possible, try to have your child preview material which will be presented the following day.** This will help her become comfortable with the vocabulary, terms and concepts which will help her get more out of the class.
- **Whenever possible, try to have him restate in his own words the assignment, directions and main points of a lesson** to his teacher, parent, or tutor to be sure he has processed the information correctly.
- **Whenever possible have your child role play what is expected in class.** This would provide opportunities to

develop strategies to help remember to do those things that are often forgotten.

- **If your child feels that he can't get himself to do schoolwork, talk to him about where he wants to be in five years.** If he still has trouble disciplining himself to do assignments and getting them in on time, accept who he is and get help from an adult or organized student. A parent, older sibling, student, teacher or tutor can help him get organized and stay on task.
- **Help your child create an inviting and comfortable study area.**
- **Follow the suggestions described in a book on study skills** such as our book *Improve Your Study Skills*.
- **Before she tries to memorize material, have her try to use visualization and drawing strategies** in order to better understand it.
- **Have your child use a weekly schedule** to be sure she leaves enough time to do assignments. (See Chapter 7.)
- **Once he understands information he needs to memorize, he needs to use chunking,** that is, dividing the material into chunks of three to five pieces of information. Consider using graphic organizers that match the material, as in our book *Improve Your Memory Skills*.

The Need for Safety

Before your children can develop self-esteem and succeed in school, they need to have their basic physical and emotional safety needs met. After all, it is difficult for them to develop positive self-images and concentrate in school if their days are spent worrying about their safety or feeling neglected. Children need to know that there will be food, a safe home, and physical help available to them. They need to feel secure. If you live in an area that is not safe, or your child's school is filled with bullies and delinquents and he feels terrorized, look into relocating your family to a safer place. If this is not possible, do whatever is necessary to ensure that your child is safe, even if that means arranging for someone, perhaps you, to take him to and from school every day.

As these safety issues can weigh heavily on children, taking a proactive approach is desirable. Small things that you do, such as dealing with your child in a consistent and predictable fashion, and big things, such as attempting to build a sense of security about his future, make a big difference. These things not only help your child feel safe, but also builds trust.

Keep alert for little signs. Most parents are always on the lookout to avoid situations that might cause their child to feel unsafe. However, because sometimes these situations sneak under their radar or cannot be avoided, it is a good idea to be sensitive to little — or not so little — signs that physical or emotional safety issues may have crept into the life of your child. Behavior changes or changes in school performance are good indicators: lack of concentration (daydreaming), acting out, lower grades, or in more severe cases, a shutting down.

Remain objective. School problems may not be caused by school issues. For example, marital problems, divorce, or a parent's loss of a job tend to cause children to feel unsafe, resulting in a decrease in school performance. If parents are not careful, they may react to the poor grades and poor school behavior — the *effect* — but miss the bigger picture — the *cause*.

Be on the lookout for little signs that physical or emotional safety issues may have crept into the life of your child.

How Does the Need for Safety Affect Children's Self-esteem?

When we insure that our children's basic needs are met, we reinforce not only their feelings of physical and emotional safety, but also their self-esteem. How is this so? By caring for their needs, we are telling them they are worthy. They are sensitive to this, and recognize that they are dependent upon their parents' care.

Think about it: as the most significant person in your child's life, if you are not available to her, who will be? Through your words and actions you convey to your child that you are both allies working toward the same goals. When there is a problem, your child needs to feel comfortable coming to you for help or guidance. Establishing this relationship should be a long-term — in fact, a lifelong — goal. This is far more important than a "C" on a spelling test or an "F" on a math test. After all, if you harangue her about each grade, she won't feel comfortable bringing a problem to you when it really counts.

> **Through your words and actions, convey to your child that you are allies working toward the same goals.**

Safety at Home

Physical Safety. Through your words and actions, convey to your child that, when at home, he is physically safe, e.g., he will have a clean, safe building to live in, with sanitary bathrooms and good food; if he is hurt or sick, those needs will be met. In short, he will get the care he requires.

Emotional Safety. In addition, children need to know their parent(s) will be in their lives, and there when they need them emotionally. Divorce can make a child afraid he will lose that security, but if he sees his parents are still trustworthy and both will still care for his needs, it will ease his anxieties somewhat.

Children need to feel safe with others as well. Your child may not spontaneously tell you how she feels when she's with other family members or with her babysitter. Ask her, and listen carefully. If she expresses some anxiety or uneasiness, don't brush aside her fear by saying something like, "Oh don't be silly. Your cousin would never hurt you—*he's* family." Instead, present yourself as an ally, as someone who will help her feel safe, someone she can turn to if she doesn't feel safe.

Children need to feel safe from physical, verbal, emotional, and social abuse. To feel secure, they cannot live in fear of ridicule or negative judgments from any source— peers, siblings, parents, teachers, or other adults. They cannot live in fear of being tormented or humiliated when they make mistakes, or sing off-key, or wake up with acne all over their faces. They cannot worry that their parents or siblings will make fun of them if they gain weight or about being punished if they inadvertently do something wrong.

And if your child *does* fail at something—for example, a school exam—instead of lecturing and punishing her, give her a hug. Even if she acts as if she doesn't care that she has failed, she does. *Then* find out what went wrong. Support her—don't put her down. She has already failed something—more negative feedback will achieve nothing.

When I explain this to parents, they typically respond, "Hug him? He never picked up a book!" or "All I ask is for her to try. I'm not asking for more. Just give me a B!"

Parents often focus on the grade itself rather than in their child's wellbeing or the reasons behind their child's poor performance.

If your child has failed a test, that means that she *did not learn* the material or *did not understand* it. She may have no idea how to learn it. *At this point, punitive action does nothing except help you to feel powerful, and your child to feel powerless, angry, and hurt.* Moreover, she will learn not to tell you about her failure next time. Instead, she will learn how to cover up, hide tests, and lie. She will *not* learn how to learn. And isn't that really your goal?

Here are some specific ideas to help your child feel physically and emotionally safe at home.

- **Use routines to help your child feel safe**

One way to help your child feel safe and secure is to keep to a set—but not rigid—routine. He needs to know what to expect, when to expect it, and what is expected of him. When you anticipate making a change in the routine, he needs to know what will happen, when it will take place, and why it is taking place. And he needs opportunities to react. He will be disturbed by change that is thrust upon him if there is no allowance for his reaction time.

Let your child know in advance about travel plans. If you or your spouse are going out for the night, away for the weekend, or leaving on a business trip, let your child know well in advance. It is frightening for him to hear suddenly that a babysitter is coming in ten minutes, or that he will be staying over at Aunt Marie's for a few days. He needs to be prepared: he needs to know where you are going, who will be taking care of him, when you are leaving, and when you will be returning.

Keep the day's schedule, including mealtimes, relatively consistent. If there are changes in her routines, she needs to know about them in advance and be given time to adjust. For example, if you are unable to make it home for an evening meal, share this with your child ahead of time, and keep her posted on the revised plans.

Inform your child about visitors. Before company comes, even if your child will be asleep beforehand, explain *who* will be coming, *why* they are coming, and *when* they will probably be leaving. If guests will be staying overnight or for several days, your child needs to know who the people are, what their relationship with you is, where they will be sleeping, how long they will be staying, and what will be expected of your child during their visit.

Prepare your child for changes in your family. If a change in your family is about to take place, try to reduce your child's anxieties by explaining what is about to happen, what plans are being made, and how it will affect her. Children need to know that unexpected changes will occur throughout their lives, and they need to learn how to handle them. But they will handle such changes better if they are able to talk about their concerns.

If you have lost your job or are changing jobs, your child will need to be prepared for the different schedule that will result, and any change in the amount of time she will see you.

If you are separating or divorcing, your child may feel abandoned, suddenly unloved, and/or somehow responsible. She will need to understand that although your family structure will change, many familiar aspects of her life will not. She will need to know where both you and her other parent will be and when she will see you both. Once one of you has moved away, she needs to see that parent's new home and be assured that it is a safe place, both for her parent and for her. She will need to know that both of you are going to be all right, and that you both still love her as much as you always have. She will need to feel that she can still tell you if she is sad or angry, and that you will attentively listen to her concerns and not brush them off because you don't want to feel guilty.

Needless to say, separation or divorce causes a tremendous upheaval in the family structure, and too often the anger, betrayal, and fear that adults feel becomes so consuming that it is difficult to focus on their children's needs. *But that is precisely the time when they need you most.* So even though it's easier said than done, you must try to put aside the anger you feel toward your spouse and remember that your child—more than anything else—needs to feel safe, loved, and supported by both of you. Alienating your child from your spouse may help *you*, and it may seem to help your child because of the peace that ensues, but for her it is a false peace. She will have an unfulfilled need; the presence and love of one of her parents is suddenly gone. She may not articulate this need to the parent who still lives with her for fear of losing that parent as well, or falling into disfavor, but the need is there nonetheless.

Chuck—Age 16

Chuck, a tall, lanky 16-year-old, had been traumatized when his dad left their family two years earlier. His grades had plummeted and his mom had taken him to see three different mental-health workers. Chuck would not open up, he was just barely passing in school, and he refused to play any sports.

When he turned 16, he started working at a local toy store and seemed to put all his energy into that job. Though his school grades were difficult to bring up, his job started giving him the stability and positive reinforcement he needed. It was at this time that I first met Chuck and his mother.

Recognizing that the problem was bigger than just academics, I told Mom that for the time being grades would not be at the top of the priority list. Have patience, I told her, and his grades will come back. The important thing is to bring stability and positive reinforcement back into his life. One of our tutors met with him weekly reducing the stress that school placed on him. Mom started going to a psychologist. We are all still hoping that someday Dad will realize how much his son needs him to be a part of his life.

What children need most in the face of such changes is as much stability as possible. They need reassurance and safety. They need to feel secure about the future and not have to worry about what will happen next.

- **Be aware of and ready to deal with the effects of circumstances beyond your control**

If the safety of your child cannot be met because of circumstances beyond your control, do your best to remedy the matter. As in the following case, outside support may be required.

Kevin — Age 8

Kevin's teacher called his mom and told her that he was doing poorly. She added that she thought Kevin could have ADHD because he spent most of his time mentally drifting off. Kevin's parents had recently been separated. His mom took him and his five-year-old brother when she left his dad because of his dad's drinking problem. Mom was angry with Dad for not seeking help. She was also angry at the court system because, for whatever reason, her husband still had custody of the boys every other weekend. Kevin told me that at times they were left alone and he had to take care of his little brother. He said that he and his brother would hide under the bed if they heard any noises. "Daddy leaves us so he could go out with his friend to drink that sweet stuff." Kevin was growing up in a world that was not safe, physically or emotionally.

In this case, the circumstances were not permanently out of control. As a result of his mom's tenacity and outside support, they were able to convince the courts that supervised visits with dad were more appropriate.

- **The working mom and the child's feeling of safety**
Volumes have been written about mothers going back to work. Many people blame working mothers for the children who have gone astray, and, in turn, mothers feel guilty when their children struggle in school. They feel that everything would be fine if they were home. But the mother's job is not what affects the children's schooling. What affects the children's schooling are two things that could be the results of mothers working: first, mothers may be exhausted, and they have neither the time nor the patience to work with their children after work; second, children may not feel as safe as they would if their mothers were home.

Some children would feel a lot better if somebody just told them, and if possible showed them, where their mothers went every day! Many children are brought to us by an au pair or babysitter, and when I ask them if they know where their mom is, they say, "At work," but they don't know where "work" is, nor do they know the telephone number where they can reach her. So the problem is not that moms are working, but that children don't feel emotionally connected to their moms when their moms are at work.

Danielle — Age 7

Danielle was having trouble in second grade. Her mom, a bright, successful corporate executive, was totally involved in her daughter's education. Her job required that she go on many business trips. Her husband was also an involved parent and felt that he could do it all. Yet, every time Mom left, Danielle would become morose and shut down in school. One day I asked Danielle where her mother was and she said, "I don't know...." She pointed toward the sky and said, "She's up there somewhere."

When her mom returned, I asked both parents to come in with Danielle. The outcome of the discussion was that I was able to provide them with a system that helped Danielle remain "connected" with her mom even when she was away. I gave Danielle a large calendar and a set of stickers. Then together we set up a list of rules.

- *Whenever Mom or Dad went away, they would put stickers on the days they would be away.*
- *They would leave the phone number of the place where they were staying with both the caregiver and with Danielle. The parents agreed on the times when they would call Danielle.*
- *Using a map or globe, they would show Danielle where they would be.*
- *Danielle would write in her journal so that when her parents called, she could share with them her important thoughts and activities.*
- *Danielle would take the journal with her to school if she wanted to.*

*The next time Mom went away, Danielle came in with
her journal and read to me where Mom was going. She
even showed me on the globe. And she began to improve
in school.*

Safety at School

Safety issues at school are basically the same as those at
home—your child needs to feel safe from physical, verbal,
emotional, and social abuse. The major difference between
home and school is that in school, there are many more
opportunities to be ridiculed, humiliated, made fun of,
picked on, physically abused, or punished. In the first place,
there are hundreds of children, many of whom are bent on
building themselves up at the expense of others. In addition,
there are a large number of adults, some of which are not
particularly sensitive to the needs of children, and a few of
whom are downright unfair, unreasonable, or worse.

While there is a safety net in place in schools, there are
lots of cracks, even gaping holes, such that children can be
made to feel terribly unsafe, physically or emotionally, in
spite of the best intentions of the adults who run schools and
classes. Lots of places and situations have "unsafe" written
all over them: the playground, lunchroom, bathrooms,
school bus, bus stop, etc. Add to this the fear of failing tests,
the fear of being left back, and a host of other academically-
related fears, and it becomes clear why many children are
in a continuous state of high anxiety or downright fear.
Needless to say, this takes a toll on academic performance.

- **Anxiety over classroom issues.**
There are many classroom issues that tend to make some
children feel unsafe. Here are some important, but not so
obvious issues, involving anxiety and arbitrary rules.

Fear of embarrassment. This is a big issue for many children. The same events that are not the slightest bit anxiety-producing for some children may be paralyzing for others. They have such a fear of being embarrassed that they are unable to achieve — or function — in school.

I always smile when parents turn to their child and say, "Just raise your hand when you don't understand something." Children have to feel *very* comfortable with the teacher and their peers to do that. Here's why. A common, knee-jerk teacher reaction is: "Jonathan, you weren't listening! I just *said* that!"

One fifth grader, Samantha, confided in me, "I won't ask her anymore. I was listening. I just don't know what she said." She didn't know what the teacher said because Samantha has a severe auditory processing problem. Her above average intelligence helps her get by, but, this year, on an almost continuous basis, she faces this conundrum. She can't ask the teacher. She can't ask her friend, because her teacher reprimands her for talking. And she doesn't understand the verbal directions. So, she does the best she can figuring things out. Sometimes she gets it and sometimes she doesn't. This is a lackluster year as far as her school grades are concerned. Her only consolation is that she'll get through this year and hopefully next year will be better.

She's not alone. This happens to everyone at some time in his academic life. I ask parents if they would raise a hand to ask a question in a large lecture hall setting. Their answer? "Are you crazy?"

Concern about missing recess. Another reason kids have anxiety in school is that they are afraid that if they don't finish the work they will have to stay in from recess. As Sven, a seven-year-old told me, "I'm afraid I'll have to sit at the wall." What does *that* mean? If he doesn't finish his morning work, while the rest of the children play during recess, he will have to sit outside at a desk—facing the wall of the building—and do his work. Sadly, this little boy processed information slowly and wasn't able to keep up. Aghast, I asked him who the teacher was. It turned out it was his *last* year's teacher. And, in spite of the fact that he was now allowed extended time and modified work due to his learning disability, and the fact that his current teacher doesn't use the "wall," the fear—*and the feeling*—did not leave. That issue had to be addressed.

Fear over being left back. Many children are afraid of being left back because they are below average in academic performance. In order to prod them along, well meaning parents and teachers occasionally use this threat as a motivating tool. Additionally, some children are convinced by parents, teachers or fellow classmates that if they don't pass the new state assessment tests they'll be left back. As a result, some of these children work themselves into a frenzy while taking the state test and, due solely to this, indeed fail. For those children, what is being tested, academic achievement or anxiety?

At the urgent request of their parents, I have personally retested some of these "failing" children using standardized achievement tests in a stress-free environment. They passed easily, allaying the fears of both parents and children.

On top of this, there is widespread confusion over the purpose of the state tests. Because they are taken by students, it appears that they are the only ones being assessed. In fact, more than the children themselves, it is the *schools* that are being assessed. (Contrary to popular belief, especially among children, they have nothing to do with children being left back.) The original intent, which, due to misconception or insufficient funding may not be implemented according to plan, is that children identified as needing additional help will *by law* get the help they need to succeed.

Consequences of arbitrary rules. While some rules work well for the majority of children, sometimes they are a terrible match for others.

Ask Three, Then Me
Amy — Age 8

Amy rarely finished her classwork, and what she did finish was done shabbily. Her mom couldn't understand why her teacher referred to her as a "problem student," so she brought her to me for an evaluation. The teacher had just told her, "I have my rules and Amy needs to follow them."

Early in the session I asked Amy what happens when the teacher tells the class to do something. Amy told me, "When the teacher tells us what to do, she goes so fast, I don't know what she says." I asked Amy why she didn't ask the teacher for help. "We're not allowed to do that. You gotta ask three, then me."

"What does that mean?" I asked Amy.

"You have to ask three kids what you are supposed to do before you are allowed to ask the teacher. I used to do that, but the kids would act annoyed and not answer me. I never ask them anymore because they started calling me stupid."

My testing found that Amy had a language-processing problem. She simply didn't understand the teacher's verbal or written instructions, and certainly couldn't understand the children who were kind enough to attempt to help her. She needed directions explained to her, then shown to her, and then, if she was still confused, to be taught through some other method.

I sent a copy of my report to her teacher, and discussed Amy's disability with her. She adjusted her rules to be more logical for Amy's situation and things improved. Sometimes, as in this case, it may appear that a child is defiant, but, in fact, something else may be afoot. Amy's case illustrates well the value of searching for the cause of an issue, and not simply focusing on the effect.

- **Excessive Teasing and Bullying from Peers**

Everyone experiences a little teasing during childhood. And while we could have lived without it, we easily brushed it off. As a result, it is easy to brush off children when they complain about being teased, or worse.

While a little bit may be part of growing up, excessive teasing or bullying makes children feel unsafe emotionally and physically, and shouldn't be ignored. Your child has the right to feel and be safe at home and at school.

If your child tells you about kids bothering him at school, look into it. Talk to the teacher, school counselor, or principal. Many times parents find out that the same child or group of children are harassing other children too. School personnel need to know about problems your child may be having with other children. In fact, they *want* to know.

There are many programs in place that address the issue of school bullies. If your school does not offer such a program, talk it up, try to get one implemented into the curriculum or through the PTA. Excessive teasing or bullying is not harmless; it is a serious—even dangerous— form of harassment. There is simply no reason that children have to live in fear of other children.

The flip side of this is the case where *your* child is the bully. If you discover this, you need to investigate the cause. Much research has been done as to why some children have the need to bully other children, and what drives them to attempt to wield power over other children. There are professionals that can help you and your child in this arena.

- **Traumatic Events**

Unfortunately, traumatic events, such as the loss of a sibling or parent, are unavoidable. Such events take their toll, to various degrees, on the home and school life of the children involved.

Jeremy — Age 9

Years ago, Jeremy was brought to me by his mom because he wasn't doing well in school. I had noticed that regardless of the topic, almost everything went back to his dad. It wasn't until the third session, however, that he provided the "detail" that his father was no longer living.

Jeremy was totally consumed by his father's tragic death; he had not yet gone far enough through the grieving process to be able to function successfully in school. Later, when I brought this up to his mom, she confirmed the loss, and provided more details. In spite of her insistence that they had worked it out together — that Jeremy was fine — I encouraged her to take him to a bereavement counselor. Fortunately, she did, and gradually, his grief became less consuming, and school issues began to abate.

Tragedies such as this affect all aspects of life. However, the effects are often most noticeable in school behavior and grades. When tragedy strikes, parents or caregivers may need to seek outside support, as with Jeremy.

These sorts of tragedies have always weighed most heavily on those directly involved. However, since 9/11, there is a perpetual cloud that hangs over all of us and is reinforced daily by a continuous stream of anxiety-producing events communicated to us by the media and directly to us as text messages and images on our cell phones and Blackberries®.

We all need to feel safe emotionally and physically. Unfortunately, in our post-9/11 world, many children and teens do not; they suffer from anxiety and depression because their basic need for safety is not being met. They cannot avoid hearing about wars, bombings, and, closer to *their* world, traumatic incidents like massacres at schools; they sense that their world has become increasingly more dangerous.

Emily — Age 10

Emily's mom was killed in the September 11, 2001 World Trade Center disaster. She was brought to see me by her grandmother because, as a result of the disaster, she was not able to function in school. In fact, she had become school phobic. Her father was doing all he could to survive. He was left with three children: a teenager, Emily, and a three-year-old. At this point, the extended family and friends were all helping to provide the emotional and physical support Dad and his children needed. In addition, Emily and her teenage brother were under the care of a psychiatrist. This sad case illustrates that sometimes the emotional safety of your child is beyond your control, and in these cases you need to search for outside support.

In Emily's case, I was able to provide assistance with the educational component, but school was obviously not the main issue. The efforts of a team consisting of her extended family, friends, psychiatrist, school counselor, and teachers helped her through the crisis, and she is now doing well—in school and out.

After the events of September 11, 2001, it took a long time for most of us to get over the reflex of looking skyward every time we heard the sound of an airliner overhead. Many of us still do. We, of course, hope attacks of this type will not recur, and the effects will continue to retreat from our everyday consciousness.

At the same time, extreme violence in schools seems to recur with some regularity, as in Columbine and the Virginia Tech massacre. I know firsthand many children who suffer from anxiety because they are afraid of bombings and killings in school. This cannot be brushed aside; these children feel downright unsafe. When the opportunity presents itself, assure your child that she is safe at school — that school personnel will protect her.

If appropriate, point out that officials have worked with parents to create an effective emergency plan, just in case. If your child is interested, provide as much information as he requires to trust that his needs will be taken care of. Encourage school officials to conduct regular disaster drills just as they do with fire drills. While many children dismiss these as silly, some find them to be a source of comfort. These measures should help them feel safer in school, so they will be more able to focus on the important issues at hand.

While controversial, consider providing your child with a cell phone, to use in case of emergency. Many children enjoy the luxury of carrying their own cell phones; just knowing that, in case of emergency, they will be able to call their parents makes them feel safer. Some schools ban cell phone use, and punish children with detention if they are caught even carrying one. This issue needs to be addressed with school personnel, police and fire departments — to hammer out reasonable policies while insuring that there is a viable plan in place in case of emergencies.

Be an active participant in the creation of a safe physical and emotional environment for your child.

Chapter 7

Achieving Goals

"My teacher said she's gonna win, but she's not. I am. I've done nothing in school for over two weeks now and I don't plan on doing anything this week either. I'll show her who's gonna win."

Frankie — Age 12

Frankie was angry. This sixth-grader sat across from me and told me that he hated his teacher. "I'm not going to do any work for her for the rest of the year," he snarled. It was November and he had gone out for recess only a couple of times since September. His teacher's policy was "No work, no recess." "She thinks she's gonna win," Frankie said, "but I know I am."

I asked Frankie what it was that he was winning. He told me that his teacher wanted him to do all his classwork. What work he didn't finish in school, he had to do as additional homework. That was the point over which he and his teacher had locked horns.

"So, let me get this straight," I said. "Your teacher wins if you break down and do your schoolwork, and you win if you continue to do nothing."

"That's right," Frankie asserted.

"I'm a little confused," I answered. "Won't you fail sixth grade if you win?"

"What?" said Frankie, looking a little perplexed.

"If you win, aren't you going to be held back?" I continued. "Is that what you want, to repeat the sixth grade?"

"No, I don't want to be left back, especially if I have to be with Mrs. Disgusting again," Frankie answered, clearly happy with the name he had given his teacher. I said nothing, and after a long pause, Frankie broke the silence. "But, I hate her and all her stupid work." He was on the verge of tears, but he managed to keep his composure.

This had become such an issue for both Frankie and his teacher that I attempted to disengage them gradually, providing each ample space to "win." I told Frankie that I understood how hard it was for him to do all that work, but it seemed to me that because he didn't want to be held back, we needed to come up with a different approach to the problem. I asked him to choose one subject for which he could do all the required work for one week. If he did all the classwork and homework in that subject, I would call his teacher to see if I could persuade her to let him begin going out for recess. A look of relief came over him.

That week he successfully completed all his math work, so I called the teacher. She noticed that not only had he done all the math work, but also that his attitude had improved. So she allowed him to go out for recess. That gesture was all he needed, so he began trying to do his other work as well.

The strategy that I used to end this stalemate involved an awareness of the importance of goals. Frankie had lost sight of important goals that might have helped provide him with direction. The immediate goal—one that was achievable within a few days—was to once again be able to participate in recess. That started the ball rolling. A longer, but still short-range goal, was to satisfactorily complete the sixth grade. Frankie could see that this was attainable in a matter of months, so it kept him focused on his task until the end of the school year. Had Frankie been older, he may have been better able to relate to and benefit from having long-range goals, such as completing high school, then college, and finally beginning a satisfying career.

Your Child's Goals

Does your child set goals for himself? What are they? Do you help him achieve them?

Goals provide children and adults alike with destinations, or targets. They are the ends. As such, they give us direction and purpose. Children who learn how to establish and attain realistic short- and long-term goals that are based on society's standards and are compatible with their own talents, desires and needs, are more likely to be successful. It is up to us adults to help them find the means that will enable them to attain their goals. This involves helping them learn how to develop strategies for confronting and overcoming obstacles in their paths. A good choice of goals provides clear and worthy targets. Thus, our job — the focus of this chapter — is to help you help your child establish and achieve his goals. Don't wait until he is grown up to teach him how to establish and attain goals. During the elementary school years it is vital that your child establishes and fulfills goals, no matter how modest. Besides being a valuable life skill, goal achievement is also an important antecedent of self-esteem.

Short-term goals are for today, next week, or the near future. They are often relatively simple. However, they are not necessarily easy to attain.

Long-term goals are targets for the future. They are often much more vague, and require additional, more complex action to attain. Some may view short-term goals as hoops to jump through in order to attain their long-term goals. For example, a child who aspires to play professional baseball (long-term goal) has to first learn how to bat and throw well (short-term goals).

> **Short-term goals are hoops to jump through in order to attain long-term goals.**

Many of the high-school kids who come to our office have impressive long-term goals. They talk about applying to top colleges and eventually becoming CEO's, doctors, or lawyers. Yet they cut classes, fail to hand in lab work and homework, and fail to study adequately for their tests. Goals are helpful only if we use them to guide ourselves to make wise decisions. Otherwise, goals are worthless.

It is surprising how many teenagers — even some seventeen and eighteen year-olds — don't see school, and required school work, as short-term goals. They don't see that doing well on homework, lab reports and tests are the hoops they need to jump through to achieve their long-term goals.

One of the first things we do when we work with kids is to focus on important short-term goals, because that is what is needed to get to the long-term goal. While we attempt to show kids where each task fits into the bigger scheme (for example, passing tests contributes to a good education, which leads to a good career which leads to a happy life), dealing exclusively with such lofty long-range goals is usually too distant and overwhelming to children. Therefore, initially we may temporarily mask everything but one short-term goal. By helping the child accomplish one homework assignment (a simple short-term goal), then another, then a lab report, then another, the child begins to see that the school tasks are not only "do-able" but they are necessary steps toward bigger and better things.

Sometimes long-term goals are meaningless to children and young teens. They are too distant, too vague, and too far from their perception planes for them to be able to relate. To many children, and some adults as well, the very thought of long-term goals is anxiety producing. They simply can't go there — supporting a future family, buying a house, dealing with having and raising children, paying for their children's college education! They need to operate in the more accessible territory of immediate short-term goals.

Help Your Child Establish Strategies to Attain Short-Term Goals

As a parent, you can help. Children often have no idea how to go about carrying out some of their goals. They have no experience on which to base their thoughts or actions. Also, the parts of their brain that would prove indispensable may not yet be developed. Thus, your child may have a goal, but he may be totally blank as to how to go about carrying it out. Parents and teachers can help considerably by working with children to formulate possible courses of action they could use to attain their goals.

- **Help your child identify short-term goals**

Try to help your child select age- and ability-appropriate goals: complete all homework for one week, or perhaps stay after school for help in math on Tuesdays, or let Mom help with spelling each night for 15 minutes. Upon satisfactory attainment of the goal, you may want to provide a suitable reward: a bowl of ice cream, a half-hour video-game session, or just a big hug!

- **Help your child develop time schedules**

Consider going with your child to an office-supply store to purchase such items as a daily planner or a PDA (personal digital assistant) that can help him to get organized. While it's not as common for children to use these as it is for adults, children need them just as much. Their lives are no less hectic than yours. And they get just as frustrated as you do when they forget things. In the long run, being organized makes them feel better about themselves.

- **Help your child organize his daily schedule, assignments, school books and notebooks**

For example, you could review his homework with him each day and together list the order in which he wants to do each assignment. Then help him allocate enough time for each assignment. However, be sure that he participates in planning his schedule with you. Resist the temptation to step in and plan your child's life, minute by minute.

Randy — Age 13

The first time Randy came to our office with his mother, I noticed that Randy was carrying a bookbag the size of a small automobile. Randy sat silently while his mom talked continuously about his disorganization. Randy seemed detached, as if the conversation had nothing to do with him, as if he had just come along for the ride.

When I asked Randy why he thought he was here, he said that he had no idea; he seemed genuinely perplexed. It was obvious that he didn't perceive that he had a problem. Mom took the lead and asked him if we could peek inside his BOOKBAG.

"It's OK with me," said Randy, a big smile emerging on his face, "but I'm warning you, opening this bag can be hazardous to your health!"

We all laughed, but Randy was right. As we opened the top flap of this overloaded bag, papers, books, notebooks, chewing gum wrappers, paper airplanes, old notices, overdue assignments, and old gym clothes tumbled out.

"Randy," I said, "you don't think there's a problem?"

"It's not my problem," he answered. "The teachers don't let you go to your locker except during lunch. And I'm afraid I'll forget things. No, I'm sure I'll forget things and my teachers will go crazy. So I cover all my bases."

Indeed he was covering all his bases. He carried the contents of his entire locker around with him all day! To help him deal with his organization problem, he had established a strategy that he believed worked for him. It did, but only in the sense that he never lost anything — evidenced by his pet phrase: "Hang in there, I'll find it, it's in here somewhere." But, it clearly wasn't working. Together, we came up with a better way.

I gave Randy a red three-ring loose-leaf book with dividers. Together we plowed through his bookbag, sorted the loose pages, and after hole-punching them, put them in their correct places: math, English, history, science, Spanish, or the paper-recycling bin. We also put into separate folders some time management sheets (see next page) and other items that he eventually would need. I then handed Randy a new assignment book and we proceeded to put together a plan of attack. After an hour of working on organization, Randy felt pretty proud of himself. I saw Randy every week after that for a few months. Not only did his grades go up, but he felt great.

TIME MANAGEMENT GRID							
Time	Mon	Tue	Wed	Thu	Fri	Sat	Sun
6:00							
7:00							
8:00							
9:00							
10:00							
11:00							
12:00							
1:00							
2:00							
3:00							
4:00							
5:00							
6:00							
7:00							
8:00							
9:00							
10:00							
11:00							

To view completed sample grids, visit our website at
www.stronglearning.com

A word about backpacks: Many children and teens today are developing neck, back and shoulder problems from carrying the weight of their school world on their backs. If this is an issue that needs attention, talk to your child's teachers or guidance counselor about how you can all help your child get to her locker between classes. Maybe there is a physical problem—for instance, her locker is too far for her to visit it between one class and another. Perhaps one or more of her teachers can have an extra set of texts in the classroom. And consider buying your child a rolling bookbag.

Organization

This kind of organization may seem simple to adults, but it is missing from the lives of many children. Kids are overwhelmed sometimes by the amount of work they seem to have, and they have difficulty organizing their assignments. As a result they might give up altogether, or begin one assignment only to skip to another before finishing. Also, it's good to encourage them to allow enough time for each assignment, since kids tend to underestimate the time they need to do it. After all, according to Murphy's Laws, everything takes longer than you think, and a kid's agenda is usually to see how quickly he can finish his homework.

- **Help your child establish priorities**
  This is most effective if you do it in a casual manner. Your child may not be as capable as you are at "prioritizing" short-term goals. She may need help seeing which activity in her day is important, which assignment she should do first, and which she might skip, if need be. You can help by telling her that it is important that she do her homework either before or after playing (depending on the child's physiological needs), or by suggesting which subject to do first. For example,

knowing that she finds math easy and that her handwriting deteriorates as she gets tired, you might suggest that she do her English homework before her math homework.

- **Try to give your child feedback regarding her progress on achieving her goals**
Positive and constructive feedback is best. For example, if your child is trying to learn the multiplication tables, the piano, or karate, say something like, "It's so impressive how you stick to it," or "You're getting better and better every day." Setting up a reward system when your child needs incentives is also a great way to provide feedback. Giving children a sticker or toy when they achieve a significant goal makes them feel good about themselves, because they're getting recognition for accomplishing a goal. Tutors often give rewards, such as ribbons, to children every time they advance to another reading level. No matter how old they are, kids love it when we adults acknowledge and reward their achievements.

- **Help your child identify the specific obstacles to the achievement of her goals**
Once your child identifies a goal, you may tell her what obstacles lie in her path. Does she want to be a firefighter? You may get her some information about the physical requirements of such a job. Does she want to drive a bus? You may tell her about the driver's test she'll need to pass.

Sometimes children have trouble attaining their short-term goals. The reasons for this vary. Some have trouble because their goals are not realistic. Some children, especially those in middle school and high school, have difficulty in classes because the classes may be inappropriate for them. While these students may be plenty bright, they simply are not developmentally ready for some of the demands of these courses. This is particularly common in accelerated math and science courses and in AP classes.

Some parents are either unable or unwilling to address the real obstacles that are preventing their children from succeeding. Instead they blame their children for being lazy, for having a low frustration level, or for giving up too quickly, and proceed to lecture and punish them when their children get poor grades. But poor grades are only effects, not causes. In such situations parents should behave as allies, not adversaries, to their children. They need to help their children by trying to identify the causes of the problems, and then trying to help them to resolve their problems.

Ways to Help Children Establish and Meet Long-Term Goals

Spend time helping your child to visualize where, and what, he wants to be. This is best done during a relaxed chat at an opportune time. Be sure to include in the conversation what he needs to do to achieve his goals. However, don't go overboard with young children; too many details may end up frightening them away from some wonderful career fields.

We know that most children have no idea what they want to become when they grow up. But by being exposed to a wide variety of career types, children and teenagers are given opportunities to set, or at least begin to think about, some real long-term goals. There are even career theme parks in various parts of the country. These provide full immersion role-playing opportunities for children in various career fields, in a highly entertaining setting. In addition, many libraries and school guidance offices have resources devoted to career opportunities. Encourage your child to visit these resources, or take her there yourself.

- **Introduce your child to varied careers that are available to him.**

  It is a good idea to be on the lookout for opportunities to discuss potential careers your child may want to consider or avoid. In fact, you and your child may sometimes be able to talk to employees themselves on their job sites. When a carpenter, plumber, or electrician is working in your house, or when you're at the dentist, or when you come across surveyors laying out a highway, it may be possible to talk to one of these professionals about the type of work she does, what she had to do or learn to get to this position, and the lifestyle she leads. Then you can point out certain traits about that career that either match or mismatch your child's personality and interests. For example, pointing out to your nocturnal child that bakers have to get up at 3:00 in the morning might eliminate that career as a long-term goal!

- **Talk about famous people.**

  Well-known historical figures and what they have provided for humankind offer good topics for conversation. Discuss with your child the accomplishments of particular scientists, inventors, explorers, authors, entertainers, and sports figures. You can find interesting and enlightening biographies in books or on television. Who knows, your child's imagination may be aroused, and career goals could develop.

- **Discuss people in the community who provide valuable services.**

  Discuss the roles of firefighters, police officers, store owners, teachers, doctors, electricians, plumbers, and so on. Many of these are people you and your child know personally. Talk about who they are and what they do. Or better yet, ask them to talk to your child about who they are and what they do.

• **Talk about family members and friends whose attributes are requisites for the work they do.**

For example, Uncle Philip is big and strong; perhaps that's why he chose to become a firefighter. Joanne, a family friend, is caring, kind, and a good organizer; maybe that's why she runs the women's shelter. Cousin John knows the city inside and out; that's one of the reasons why he's a good assignment editor for the TV station.

• **Talk to your child about using a self-checklist.**

Encourage your child to use self-evaluations. How am I doing? This is a good test of a successful individual: one who can judge his own worth without depending on another's evaluation. To do this, the child writes down his goals. Then he puts them in order to see what needs to be done first, second, etc. to accomplish these goals. Next, he puts dates next to each goal to be sure he knows when he needs to meet the goal.

Help Your Child Create Positive Target Images

It is good for children to visualize idealized images and then to learn how to develop their own goals. This way, like their role models, they can succeed. It's your job to be one such role model for your child, and to help him find other role models.

Ask your child what kind of person he would like to be when he grows up. His answer might very well be that he wants to be like you! But if his answer is some violent arch-villain of a comic super-hero, don't panic. Either way, he needs more potential role models from which to choose. You're the one who can expose him to them firsthand, or point them out to him. It's your job to be a role model for your child, and to help him find other role models.

Suggestions for helping to visualize role models

- **Expose your child to theater, art, music, sporting events, movies, lectures, family outings, and other stimulating experiences.** Through exposure to the world beyond the family setting, your child is provided with additional potential role models to emulate. This can be done by way of trips, literary or cyberspace "journeys," DVD or CD-ROM programs, walks into town, or conversations.
- **Share with your child your own occupational domain.** Yours may be a field in which your youngster expresses interest. The success of such visits depends on the appropriateness of the workplace and the planning that precedes it. The payoff comes in the opportunity for parent and child to share fresh perspectives on many levels. (Note: Be careful not to force the issue. It's risky to "groom" a child for the same occupation as yours or to take over your business. That might be your dream, but it may not be your child's.)
- **Play Twenty Questions to attempt to identify famous people.** You will start to see a pattern emerge in whom your child names. This pattern might reveal more about whom your child looks up to than you would think.
- **Help your child to write a letter to a famous or not-so-famous person (past or present) that he admires.** It feels good to express appreciation to someone for his or her contribution to society.

Remember, in a sense, goals are like rudders on ships. Realistic short- and long-term goals help us to steer our lives. As a parent, help your child become a good navigator.

> **Goals are like rudders on ships. Realistic short- and long-term goals help us to steer our lives.**

Conclusion

Hopefully, you have had some questions answered and some problems solved by reading *Why Bad Grades Happen to Good Kids*. Since being a parent is not easy, you may still have some unanswered issues. If so, you may need to contact a professional to help sort out the problem.

For more information, we hope you will visit our website *www.stronglearning.com*.

In the meantime, remember the following hints:

- Keep school in perspective.
- Be patient.
- Promote positive self-esteem and good character in your child because they are essential to growth and development. Do this by accepting, supporting and encouraging your child — through your words and actions — and by having him feel he is part of a family, a school and a community.
- Give your children the kind of respect you expect from them.
- Be a good role model. Parents' behavior affects their child's development, in school and out.
- Be a trustworthy parent because trustworthy parents promote trustworthy children.
- Let your child know his parents are on his team.

- Give your child appropriate responsibility because it is a prerequisite to growth and development and school success.
- Help your children become responsible by establishing rules that are fair, make sense and are easy for children to follow.
- When your child breaks a rule, find out why.
- Help your child develop decision-making skills, because learning how to make decisions in various situations gives children control over their lives, and encourages them to be responsible for their behavior — all of which is integral to the lifestyle of the successfully functioning student and adult.
- Be sure all your child's basic needs are met.
- Deal with your child in a consistent, predictable fashion because it helps your child feel safe and builds trust.
- Help your child establish strategies to attain short and long-term goals to help steer her life today and in the future.

Remember, young people who feel valued and important can succeed in school and, as grown-ups, contribute responsibly to society. Children need to be accepted by their parents for whom they are, they need to be supported in areas where they can, and be loved, even when they bring home a less than perfect grade.

> **Learn who your child is, rejoice in his strengths, and look forward to lots of good things happening to your good kid.**

References

Adolescent Attachment to Parents and Friends in Relation
     to Aspects of Self-Esteem. Paterson, Janis; and
     Others. Journal of Youth and Adolescence, v24 n3
     p 365-76 Jun 1995

ACA Releases First National Survey: Special Report.
     Miller, John A. Camping Magazine, v67 n4 p34-35
     Mar-Apr 1995. Theme issue topic: "Human Behavior."

Barkley, R.A. (2005). ADD and the nature of self-control. New
     York: The Guilford Press.

Beane, J. A. (1991, September). Sorting out the self-esteem con-
     troversy. *Educational Leadership*, 25-9.

Botvin, G. J. & Dusenbury, L. (1987) Substance abuse preven-
     tion and the promotion of competence. (Original Re-
     search). New York: Cornell University Medical College,
     Dept. of Public Health, Laboratory of Health Behavior
     Research.

California Commission to Promote self-esteem, and Personal
     and Social Responsibility. (1989). Esteem (Legislative
     Counsel's Digest, Assembly Bill No. 3659). California:
     Government Printing Office.

Canfield, J. (1990, September). Improving students' self-esteem.
     Educational Leadership, 48-50.

Coopersmith, S. (1981). *The antecedents of self-esteem.* California: Consulting Psychologists Press, Inc.

Domain Importance and Involvement: Relations between Domain Self-Concepts and General Self-Esteem in Preadolescence. Forte, Ellen E.; Vispoel, Walter P. Apr 1995. 41p.; Paper presented at the Annual Meeting of the American Educational Research Association (San Francisco, CA, April 18-22, 1995).

Erikson, E. 1964. *Childhood and Society,* 2nd. ed. New York: W.W. Norton.

Erikson, E. (1982). The life cycle completed: A review. New York: W.W. Norton.

Evaluating the Nature of Perceived Support and Its Relation to Perceived Self-Worth in Adolescents. Robinson, Nancy S. Journal of Research on Adolescence, v5 n2 p253-80 1995

Ginsburg, H. & Opper, S. (1969). **Piaget's theory of intellectual development**. Englewood Cliffs: Prentice-Hall, Inc.

Harter, S. (in press). Causes and consequences of low self-esteem in children and adolescents. In R.F. Baumeister (Ed.), Self-esteem: The puzzle of low self-regard. Denver: University of Denver.

Harter, S. (1989). Causes, correlates, and the functional role of global self-worth: A life-span perspective. Perceptions of competence and incompetence across the life-span. New Haven: Yale University Press.

Ianni, F. A.J. (1989) The Search for Structure: A Report on American Youth Today. New York: The Free Press.

Jensen, E. (1998). Teaching with the brain in mind. Virginia: As sociation for Supervision and Curriculum Development.

Juhasz, A. M. (1989, Fall). Significant others and self-esteem: Methods for determining who and why. Adolescence, 24 (95), 581-94.

Kagan, J. (1984). *The nature of the child*. New York: Basic.

Legislative Counsel's Digest. (1986). California commission to promote self-esteem, and personal and social responsibility. (Assembly Bill No. 3659). California: Government Printing Office.

Levine, M. (2002). *A mind at a time*. New York: Simon and Schuster.

Luster, T., McAdoo & Pipes, H. (1995). Factors related to self esteem among African American youths: A Secondary Analysis of the High/Scope Perry Preschool Data.

Maslow, A.H. (1968). *Toward a psychology of being*. Princeton, MA: Van Nostrand.

McKay, M. & Fanning, P. (1987) Self-esteem. New York: MFJ Books. Parent-Child Attachment Working Models and Self-Esteem in Adolescence.

McCormick, Cynthia B.; Kennedy, Janice H. Journal of Youth and Adolescence, v23 n1 p1-18 Feb 1994

Rogers, C. (1961). *On becoming a person*. Boston: Houghton Mifflin.

Shaywitz, S., M.D. ((2003). *Overcoming Dyslexia*. New York: Alfred A. Knopf.

Sprenger, M. (1999), Learning and memory, the brain in action. Virginia: Association for Supervision and Curriculum Development.

Strauch, B. (2003). *The primal teen*. New York: Anchor Books.

Sylvester, R. (1995). A celebration of neurons. Virginia: Association for Supervision and Development.

Sprinthall, N. A. & Sprinthall, R. (1990). *Educational psychology — developmental approach (5th ed.)*. New York: McGraw Hill. "The Relationship of Self-Esteem to Grades, Achievement Scores, and Other Factors Critical to School Success."

Wiggins, James D.; And Others, School Counselor, v41 n4 p239-44 Mar 1994

Index

List of Case Studies

List of Case Studies

About the Authors

Linda & Alvin Silbert have dedicated over thirty-five years to the growth and enhancement of children's intellectual, emotional, and social development. They have written over forty books, for children in kindergarten through college, which have sold over one million copies. They lecture and lead workshops about how to help children succeed in school and beyond. They have appeared on radio and television throughout the U.S. & Canada. They continue to collaborate as writers, educational therapists, and directors of Strong Learning Centers based in Chappaqua, New York. They have two grown children and two grandchildren. The Silberts live in the suburbs of New York.